CL

YOUR BODY
How It Works

The Circulatory System

YOUR BODY How It Works

The Circulatory System

Susan Whittemore, Ph.D.
Professor of Biology
Keene State College, Keene, N.H.

Introduction by
Denton A. Cooley, M.D.
President and Surgeon-in-Chief
of the Texas Heart Institute
Clinical Professor of Surgery at the
University of Texas Medical School, Houston, Texas

CHELSEA HOUSE
PUBLISHERS
A Haights Cross Communications Company
Philadelphia

CHELSEA HOUSE PUBLISHERS
VP, NEW PRODUCT DEVELOPMENT Sally Cheney
DIRECTOR OF PRODUCTION Kim Shinners
CREATIVE MANAGER Takeshi Takahashi
MANUFACTURING MANAGER Diann Grasse

Staff for The Circulatory System
EDITOR Beth Reger
PRODUCTION EDITOR Megan Emery
PHOTO EDITOR Sarah Bloom
SERIES & COVER DESIGNER Terry Mallon
LAYOUT 21st Century Publishing and Communications, Inc.

www.chelseahouse.com

First Printing

1 3 5 7 9 8 6 4 2

Library of Congress Cataloging-in-Publication Data

Whittemore, Susan.
  The circulatory system / Susan Whittemore.
    v. cm. -- (Your body, how it works)
  Includes index.
  Contents: Gravity and the human circulatory system -- Overview of the
human circulatory system -- The composition of blood -- Oxygen transport:
the role of hemoglobin -- Anatomy of the circulatory system -- Pumping
blood: how the heart works -- The control of blood pressure and distribution
-- Circulatory responses to hemorrhage and exercise.
  ISBN 0-7910-7626-1
  1. Cardiovascular system--Juvenile literature. 2. Blood--Circulation--Juve-
nile literature. [1. Circulatory system. 2. Blood.] I. Title. II. Series.
  QP103.W458 2004
  612.1--dc22
                           2003025584

Table of Contents

Introduction

The human body is an incredibly complex and amazing structure. At best, it is a source of strength, beauty, and wonder. We can compare the healthy body to a well-designed machine whose parts work smoothly together. We can also compare it to a symphony orchestra in which each instrument has a different part to play. When all of the musicians play together, they produce beautiful music.

From a purely physical standpoint, our bodies are made mainly of water. We are also made of many minerals, including calcium, phosphorous, potassium, sulfur, sodium, chlorine, magnesium, and iron. In order of size, the elements of the body are organized into cells, tissues, and organs. Related organs are combined into systems, including the musculoskeletal, cardio-vascular, nervous, respiratory, gastrointestinal, endocrine, and reproductive systems.

Our cells and tissues are constantly wearing out and being replaced without our even knowing it. In fact, much of the time, we take the body for granted. When it is work-ing properly, we tend to ignore it. Although the heart beats about 100,000 times per day and we breathe more than 10 million times per year, we do not normally think about these things. When something goes wrong, however, our bodies tell us through pain and other symptoms. In fact, pain is a very effective alarm system that lets us know the body needs attention. If the pain does not go away, we may need to see a doctor. Even without medical help, the body has an amazing ability to heal itself. If we cut ourselves, the blood clotting system works to seal the cut right away, and the immune defense system sends out special blood cells that are programmed to heal the area.

During the past 50 years, doctors have gained the ability to repair or replace almost every part of the body. In my own field of cardiovascular surgery, we are able to open the heart and repair its valves, arteries, chambers, and connections. In many cases, these repairs can be done through a tiny "keyhole" incision that speeds up patient recovery and leaves hardly any scar. If the entire heart is diseased, we can replace it altogether, either with a donor heart or with a mechanical device. In the future, the use of mechanical hearts will probably be common in patients who would otherwise die of heart disease.

Until the mid-twentieth century, infections and contagious diseases related to viruses and bacteria were the most common causes of death. Even a simple scratch could become infected and lead to death from "blood poisoning." After penicillin and other antibiotics became available in the 1930s and '40s, doctors were able to treat blood poisoning, tuberculosis, pneumonia, and many other bacterial diseases. Also, the introduction of modern vaccines allowed us to prevent childhood illnesses, smallpox, polio, flu, and other contagions that used to kill or cripple thousands.

Today, plagues such as the "Spanish flu" epidemic of 1918–19, which killed 20 to 40 million people worldwide, are unknown except in history books. Now that these diseases can be avoided, people are living long enough to have long-term (chronic) conditions such as cancer, heart failure, diabetes, and arthritis. Because chronic diseases tend to involve many organ systems or even the whole body, they cannot always be cured with surgery. These days, researchers are doing a lot of work at the cellular level, trying to find the underlying causes of chronic illnesses. Scientists recently finished mapping the human genome, which is a set of coded "instructions" programmed into our cells. Each cell contains 3 billion "letters" of this code. By showing how the body is made, the human genome will help researchers prevent and treat disease at its source, within the cells themselves.

The body's long-term health depends on many factors, called risk factors. Some risk factors, including our age, sex, and family history of certain diseases, are beyond our control. Other important risk factors include our lifestyle, behavior, and environment. Our modern lifestyle offers many advantages but is not always good for our bodies. In western Europe and the United States, we tend to be stressed, overweight, and out of shape. Many of us have unhealthy habits such as smoking cigarettes, abusing alcohol, or using drugs. Our air, water, and food often contain hazardous chemicals and industrial waste products. Fortunately, we can do something about most of these risk factors. At any age, the most important things we can do for our bodies are to eat right, exercise regularly, get enough sleep, and refuse to smoke, overuse alcohol, or use addictive drugs. We can also help clean up our environment. These simple steps will lower our chances of getting cancer, heart disease, or other serious disorders.

These days, thanks to the Internet and other forms of media coverage, people are more aware of health-related matters. The average person knows more about the human body than ever before. Patients want to understand their medical conditions and treatment options. They want to play a more active role, along with their doctors, in making medical decisions and in taking care of their own health.

I encourage you to learn as much as you can about your body and to treat your body well. These things may not seem too important to you now, while you are young, but the habits and behaviors that you practice today will affect your physical well-being for the rest of your life. The present book series, YOUR BODY: HOW IT WORKS, is an excellent introduction to human biology and anatomy. I hope that it will awaken within you a lifelong interest in these subjects.

Denton A. Cooley, M.D.
President and Surgeon-in-Chief
of the Texas Heart Institute
Clinical Professor of Surgery at the
University of Texas Medical School, Houston, Texas

1

Gravity and the Human Circulatory System

After more than 30 years of space travel, scientists have learned that almost every body system is affected by life in space. Astronauts lose muscle mass in their legs and lose bone mass due to demineralization. The loss of minerals such as calcium from the bones can cause kidney stones and eventually lead to osteoporosis and spinal fractures similar to those seen in elderly people. Space travel also adversely affects the human circulatory system and, as we will see, could make space travel a very dangerous activity.

THE EFFECTS OF MICROGRAVITY ON HUMAN CIRCULATION

The human **circulatory system**, also known as the **cardiovascular system**, is designed to efficiently deliver blood, and the nutrients and oxygen it carries, to all of the body's tissues. In this way, all of our body's tissues rely on the circulatory system and its function is critical to life. It is no wonder that there are many physiologists, scientists who study how the body works, who specialize in the human circulatory system. It may surprise you to learn, however, that there is an entire field of physiology, known as space physiology, devoted to understanding how the human body functions in space.

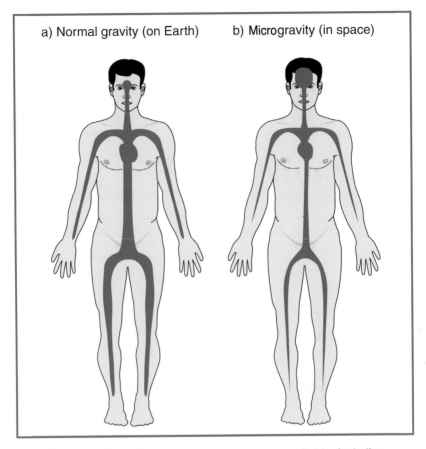

Figure 1.1 In the microgravity of space, body fluids, including blood, shift to the upper regions of the body, eventually leading to a reduction in blood volume. Upon return to Earth's gravitational field, the majority of the blood volume shifts back into the lower body regions and, because the volume is reduced, blood pressure drops too low. Under such circumstances, standing might lead to dizziness.

In the absence of gravity, also known as **microgravity** (or zero gravity), body fluids, including blood, shift away from the lower body and into the upper body, causing blood to pool in the chest and head (Figure 1.1). This fluid shift affects the heart, which becomes enlarged to deal with the excess blood flow. Over time, this fluid shift is perceived by the body to be excess volume, causing certain responses that reduce the blood volume significantly.

Space physiologists observing these changes have two basic questions to ask. First, how does this blood-volume shift and eventual reduction affect an astronaut's health and ability to carry out assigned tasks? Second, are these effects reversible upon return to Earth or will there be any long-term consequences of space travel on an astronaut's health?

At some point in your life, you have probably jumped out of bed quickly and felt momentarily dizzy. Our circulatory system makes constant adjustments to our blood pressure whenever we change our posture. When a person stands up quickly, gravity draws his or her blood to the large veins in the legs and abdomen and away from the upper body and brain, causing the blood pressure to drop and making the person feel light-headed. Usually, the circulatory system immediately makes adjustments in blood pressure to restore flow to the upper body and counteract the effects of gravity.

After two weeks of space flights, 20% of returning astronauts experience difficulty standing up without getting dizzy, a condition known as **orthostatic intolerance**. This condition is the same as when a person stands up too quickly, as described in the previous paragraph. In a study conducted by NASA, the longer an astronaut remains in space, the greater the risk of orthostatic intolerance.

Space physiologists have also noted that astronauts have an increased incidence of **arrhythmias,** or abnormal heart beats, in space. The direct cause of this response is unknown. Astronauts also suffer from **anemia**, or a reduced number of circulating red blood cells, the cells that carry oxygen. The space-related anemia appears to be due to a diminished production of new red blood cells rather than an increase in red-blood-cell destruction. Scientists studying space-related anemia use prolonged bed rest on Earth, which also results in anemia, as a model for their investigations.

Another factor affected by the circulatory system's response to near-zero gravity is the effectiveness of medical drugs.

Many of the drugs that are delivered to their action sites by the circulatory system do not appear to work as well in space as they do on Earth. Space physiologists are not sure whether this effect is the result of a delivery problem due to the circulatory adjustments to space or due to an increase in the rate of drug elimination by the liver and kidney, two organs that become enlarged in microgravity.

TOO MUCH GRAVITY? THE EFFECTS OF HYPERGRAVITY ON HUMAN CIRCULATION

Humans can also find themselves in situations where they experience **hypergravity**, or gravity greater than that on Earth. For example, fighter pilots experience up to nine times the normal weight of gravity when they perform certain maneuvers in their aircraft. The amount of gravitational, or G-, force experienced by a fighter pilot can drive the blood *away* from critical organs such as the brain, lungs, and heart, leading to fatigue, blackouts, and sometimes even death. G-suits were developed to counteract the effects of hyper-gravity (see the box entitled "Inspired By The Dragonfly" on following page).

Recently, physicians have become alarmed about the trend for amusement parks to develop faster and steeper roller coasters and other rides that effectively expose the average, untrained human body to ever-increasing gravitational forces. How do scientists study the effects of gravitational force on the human body? The Ames Center for Gravitational Biology has its own "amusement park" for just that purpose, including a human centrifuge that can generate gravitational forces up to 20 times that of Earth!

WHAT THESE STUDIES TELL US

It may have surprised you to learn in this chapter that there are scientists who specialize in investigating the effects of changes in gravity on the human body. Are the results of their studies only of value to NASA or the military? Most physiologists would argue that the knowledge gained from such experiments benefits all of us, because in the process we learn a great deal about how the human body works on Earth, both in health and with disease. When scientists investigate the effects of either increasing or decreasing amounts of gravitational pull on the

INSPIRED BY THE DRAGONFLY

G-suits were designed to protect fighter pilots from the effects of standard jet maneuvers that resulted in greatly increased gravitational force, or hypergravity. Hypergravity drives blood into the extremities and away from the brain, heart, and lungs, causing extreme fatigue, blackouts, and possibly death. Using compressed air, the original G-suit, developed in the 1940s, squeezed the lower body to drive blood back toward the heart.

The technology behind these suits has remained essentially the same during the past 50 years. Although these suits are beneficial, fighter pilots return from their flights exhausted and often need help getting out of their cockpits. It takes the G-suits a few seconds to respond to changes in gravitational force because air has to be pumped into the suit. Repeated exposure to even a few seconds of the blood shift appears to cause fatigue.

Andreas Reinhard designed a new G-suit after researching the dragonfly, the only animal that can withstand 30 times the gravitational force of Earth while flying. Because the circulatory system of the dragonfly is encased in fluid, Reinhard designed a fluid-filled suit that could absorb the increased gravitational force associated with flight maneuvers. As the pilot begins a downward spiral, for example, the water channels compress and prevent the blood from shifting.

Fighter pilots who have tested these new G-suits report that they found it easier to breathe and communicate while flying and returned less fatigued. It is likely that these new G-suits will be used in the near future.

human body, they learn how our body systems have evolved to deal with continuous exposure to normal levels of gravity that accompany life on Earth. For example, studies of space-related anemia have helped physiologists better understand diseases such as Shy-Drager syndrome, which has similar symptoms to those associated with this kind of anemia.

In the remaining chapters of this book, you will explore how the human circulatory system functions. You will read an overview of the entire system, including how it interacts with the respiratory system to deliver oxygen to the respiring tissues. You will explore the properties and functions of blood, the anatomy and physiology of the heart, and the structure and function of the blood vessels. In addition, you will examine the homeostatic mechanisms that keep your heart beating and your blood flowing in response to changes in the oxygen needs of the body.

2

Overview of the Human Circulatory System

The human **circulatory system** consists of the heart—a muscular pumping mechanism—and a closed system of vessels—arteries, veins, and capillaries. The heart pumps oxygen- and nutrient-rich blood contained within the system around a circuit of vessels, supplying all of the body's tissues with the blood that is critical for sustaining life.

The process of **diffusion**, the random movement of molecules from a region of higher concentration to a region of lower concentration, is not fast enough to support the oxygen and nutrient demands of a large multicellular organism like a human. Diffusion only works over very short distances. While humans do rely on diffusion between the blood and the atmosphere in the lungs, and between the blood and the cells in the capillaries, the delivery of blood to these exchange sites must be rapid and efficient. For these reasons, blood is transported throughout the human body by the process of **bulk flow**. Through this process, air and blood move from regions of higher pressure to regions of lower pressure. In the human circulatory system, the heart is the pump that generates the pressure gradients that drive the bulk flow of blood. Such a system allows for the rapid transport of molecules in respiratory gases and nutrients over long distances, in order to reach all of the body's tissues.

THE STRUCTURE AND FUNCTION
OF THE CIRCULATORY SYSTEM

The circulatory system consists of the blood, a fluid connective tissue, contained completely within a circular vascular system (or network of blood vessels) that is connected to a pump, the heart. The heart and its system of delivering blood is composed of two separate circuits. The **pulmonary circuit** (supplied by the right side of the heart), receives blood returning to the heart from the body and pumps it to the lungs. This circuit serves to exchange carbon dioxide in the blood with oxygen from the lungs (Figure 2.1). The **systemic circuit** (supplied by the left side of the heart) takes the freshly oxygenated blood and delivers it to the entire body.

In both circuits, the blood travels through a series of blood vessels. Blood is pumped out of the heart into large muscular arteries that branch into smaller arteries, then arterioles, followed by intricate networks of tiny capillaries. The capillaries are the sites of exchange between the blood and nearby cells. After leaving the capillaries, the blood is collected into venules and then veins of increasing size, before being returned to the heart. In both systems, arteries take blood *away from* the heart, and veins bring blood *toward* the heart.

FOLLOWING A RED BLOOD CELL: THE FLOW OF
BLOOD THROUGH THE CIRCULATORY SYSTEM

One of the best ways to understand the design of the human circulatory system is to take a ride with a red blood cell through the entire circuit. Let's start in the left ventricle, the larger muscular chamber of the left side of the heart. When the heart beats, the red blood cell gets forcibly ejected from the left ventricle into the aorta. From there, the blood cell travels into one of many large arteries that branch into progressively smaller arteries. Hence, each vessel the red blood cell enters will eventually lead to multiple exit points as it branches. Soon, the red blood cell moves from a small systemic artery into a systemic arteriole with a smaller diameter. The arteriole leads to a

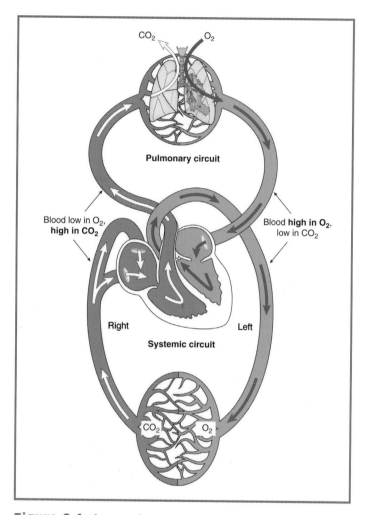

Figure 2.1 An overview of the human circulatory system is illustrated here. This system is divided into two separate circuits: the pulmonary circuit, which carries blood to the lungs for oxygenation, and the systemic circuit, which supplies the entire body with oxygenated blood. The blood within these vessels and heart is colored blue when it has reduced oxygen content and red when fully oxygenated. Trace the route of a red blood cell as it completes one entire circuit through this system. Note that for both the pulmonary and systemic circuits, arteries carry blood that is moving away from the heart, while veins carry blood that is returning to the heart.

systemic capillary bed in some tissue in the body where the vessels are so small that the red blood cell can barely squeeze through.

In this systemic capillary, the red blood cell gives up some of its load of oxygen (O_2) molecules to nearby cells for use in the process of cellular respiration. Carbon dioxide (CO_2), a waste product of cellular respiration, diffuses from these cells into the blood cell. After this exchange of gases, the blood cell enters a venule, then a small vein, and then a larger vein. Eventually, the blood cell reaches the large veins that deposit the oxygen-poor blood into the right atrium. This is the end of the systemic circuit.

The pulmonary circuit (where the red blood cell once again becomes oxygenated) begins when the blood is pumped from the right atrium into the right ventricle and leaves via the pulmonary arteries to travel to the lungs. Again, there is a significant degree of branching of both the larger and then the smaller pulmonary arteries. The red blood cell progresses from a small pulmonary arteriole into a pulmonary capillary, which is wrapped around a small portion of the lung surface. The carbon dioxide diffuses out of the capillary and into the air within the lung while oxygen is diffusing in the opposite direction and binding to the **hemoglobin** molecules packed within the red blood cells (hemoglobin is a protein that helps red blood cells carry oxygen). Once again, pulmonary venules and then successively larger veins collect the blood as it leaves its capillary bed. Soon after entering one of the large pulmonary veins, the blood cell is deposited into the left atrium and finally the left ventricle, where it first began its journey.

There is no rest for the red blood cell. For blood to accomplish its function, it must remain in motion. As soon as it becomes stationary, its store of oxygen and nutrients quickly becomes depleted and the cell becomes saturated with waste products. Other critical functions, described in the next chapter, also become disrupted. To keep the body's blood in motion, the heart pumps about 8,000 liters of blood per day. This is equivalent to 4,000 regular two-liter soda bottles!

It is difficult to say how quickly an individual blood cell will travel through the circulatory system. It would depend on which specific body tissue a specific blood cell circulates through. Flow through individual organs and tissues varies from minute to minute based on the changing oxygen demands of tissues and on the type and degree of human activity taking place at that time. The total flow of blood through the system remains fairly constant and is typically about 5.25 liters/minute, close to the total volume of blood contained within the system.

Figure 2.2 shows how the rate of blood flow is affected by blood vessel type. Flow is far more rapid in the arteries than it is within the capillaries. Arteries are delivery vessels, while capillaries are sites of exchange, a process that requires time.

CONNECTIONS

The human circulatory system is designed to rapidly and efficiently transport blood to all regions of the body. Blood is contained under pressure within a vascular system composed of several types of blood vessels. The human circulatory system is composed of two separate circuits: the pulmonary circuit, which carries blood to the lungs to be oxygenated, and the systemic circuit, which supplies the entire body with oxygenated blood.

Blood carries oxygen and nutrients needed by the body's respiring tissues. Blood also transports cellular wastes to elimination sites. Many of the other important functions of blood and the human circulatory system are addressed in the next chapter. Although diffusion drives the exchange of gases and molecules in the capillaries, blood must remain in rapid motion to perform its diverse functions. The heart serves as a pump, generating the blood pressures needed to achieve bulk flow of this fluid. The four-chambered heart of

VESSEL	TYPICAL LUMEN DIAMETER	VELOCITY
BLOOD VELOCITY IN THE SYSTEMIC CIRCUIT		
AORTA	2.5 cm	1,200 mm/sec
ARTERIOLES	20-50 μm	15 mm/sec
CAPILLARIES	5-9 μm	0.4 mm/sec
VENULES	20 μm	5 mm/sec
INFERIOR VENA CAVA	3 cm	80 mm/sec

Figure 2.2 The rate of blood flow varies within the different blood vessels. The smaller the interior, or lumen, diameter, the slower the rate of flow. (Note: 1 cm = 0.01 m and 1 μm = 0.000001 m.)

humans consists of two pumps that beat as one. The right side of the heart provides the pressure to propel blood through the pulmonary circuit, while the left side of the heart forces blood to flow through the systemic circuit.

3

The Composition of Blood

Blood can convey a lot of information about a person. It contains a person's unique genetic profile. It can signal the presence of certain diseases, such as cancer, and indicate deficiencies or chemical imbalances in the body, such as iron deficiency. An individual's risk of suffering heart disease and whether or not a person has been exposed to a toxic substance can be determined from a blood sample. Blood levels of alcohol or other drugs can indicate a person's degree of impairment for performing certain tasks, such as driving. No other bodily tissue can provide such a range of information about a person's health.

BLOOD IS A FLUID TISSUE

Blood plays an important role in many functions of the circulatory system. It transports nutrients from their site of absorption in the digestive tract to the cells that require these nutrients. Blood carries waste products from the cells' activities to the kidneys for disposal from the body. It distributes hormones to organs that the endocrine system uses to coordinate physiological functions in our bodies. Red blood cells transport oxygen from our lungs to our cells, while white blood cells are important in fighting infection. Our blood carries **clotting factors** and **platelets** to help prevent the blood loss that often occurs with injury. Blood also carries heat generated in the body core to other parts of the body, and distributes water and electrolytes to all of our tissues.

The tissues of the body can be classified into four major types: epithelial, muscular, nervous, and connective. Epithelial tissues, such as the outer layers of the skin and the innermost layer of our digestive system, provide barriers between such organs and their environment, among other important functions. Nervous tissue is involved in sensing and responding to our internal and external environments and supports communication and coordination among different organ systems. Muscle tissue is involved in movement of the body, movement of blood around the body, and movement of food through the digestive system. Connective tissue represents a diverse group of tissues, including the bones and cartilage of the skeletal system, the collagen layer of the skin, fat tissue surrounding organs, and the blood.

Blood is a fluid and is classified as a connective tissue because it possesses cells (red and white blood cells) that are surrounded by an extensive extracellular matrix component known as the plasma. Although many other connective tissues play important structural and protective roles, blood functions to distribute a wide variety of substances that are critical to life.

THE CELLS OF THE BLOOD

If we take a sample of whole blood and spin it down in a centrifuge to separate its major components, we would obtain a sample similar to the one shown in Figure 3.1. At the top of the centrifuged blood sample is a fluid called **plasma** that represents about 55% of the total volume. Beneath that is a whitish layer called the buffy coat. This layer contains **leukocytes**, or white blood cells, which fight diseases, and platelets, which are important in slowing blood loss. This layer constitutes less than 1% of the total volume of blood. The remaining nearly 45% of blood consists of red blood cells, also called **erythrocytes**, which carry oxygen to the tissues. The buffy coat and erythrocytes are the blood's solid components.

Red Blood Cells

Red blood cells are unusual because they are so structurally simple. Mature red blood cells do not have a nucleus and, therefore, have no means of activating genes and producing gene products as needed. They have no ribosomes, mitochondria, or

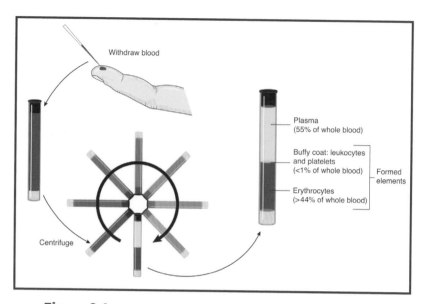

Figure 3.1 When a sample of whole blood is spun in a centrifuge, the solid components settle to the bottom of the tube. Red blood cells (erythrocytes) constitute about 45% of the volume of blood. The white blood cells (leukocytes) and platelets represent less than 1% of the volume and are present in the buffy coat on top of the red blood cells. The remaining 55% of the volume is plasma, the liquid matrix surrounding the blood cells.

many of the other organelles that typical animal cells have. Each red blood cell is a package of hemoglobin molecules, the respiratory proteins that carry oxygen in the blood. The biconcave shape of the red blood cell allows it to fold and squeeze through small capillaries and provides a large surface area for oxygen diffusion. The structure and function of the hemoglobin it contains will be addressed in Chapter 4.

Red Blood Cell Production
Because red blood cells cannot undergo cellular reproduction or repair, they typically live for 120 days. When a red blood cell starts to wear out, it is removed from circulation by the spleen. As a result, every day a human must generate 250 billion replacement cells from his or her bone marrow.

The process of blood cell formation is called **hematopoiesis** and occurs in bone marrow. Pluripotent (able to form most tissue) **hematopoietic stem cells** are undifferentiated cells, present in the bone marrow, that have the capacity to become any of the different blood cell types. When stimulated to divide by certain growth factors, these stem cells can either replace themselves with two identical daughter pluripotent stem cells, or they can become committed to a certain developmental pathway.

As seen in Figure 3.2, once an uncommitted stem cell differentiates into a myeloblast, this stem cell can give rise to all other blood cell types. We can also see that lymphoblasts give rise to lymphocytes.

In the bone marrow, immature red blood cells contain all of the organelles that typical cells contain. During the maturation process, red blood cells lose many of their major organelles before they enter the circulatory system. Red-blood-cell production is stimulated by the hormone **erythropoietin**. This hormone is synthesized by the kidney and travels via the bloodstream to the bone marrow, where it binds to hormone receptors and promotes the production of mature red blood cells.

All cells require energy in the form of adenosine triphosphate (ATP) to perform their functions. Because a mature red blood cell does not have a nucleus, ribosomes, or mitochondria, it cannot produce ATP as other cells do. Red blood cells, however, do not require as much ATP as typical cells do, but they do require energy for membrane transport processes and the maintenance of a proper internal environment. Red blood cells have enzymes of glycolysis that produce ATP in sufficient quantities to meet the lower ATP demands of these important cells.

The volume of whole blood occupied by red blood cells is called the **hematocrit** and is typically about 45%. If an individual's hematocrit starts to decrease, the resulting decrease in the oxygen-carrying capacity of the blood is sensed by the kidney, which releases more erythropoietin, the hormone involved in red blood cell production (Figure 3.3). Decreased

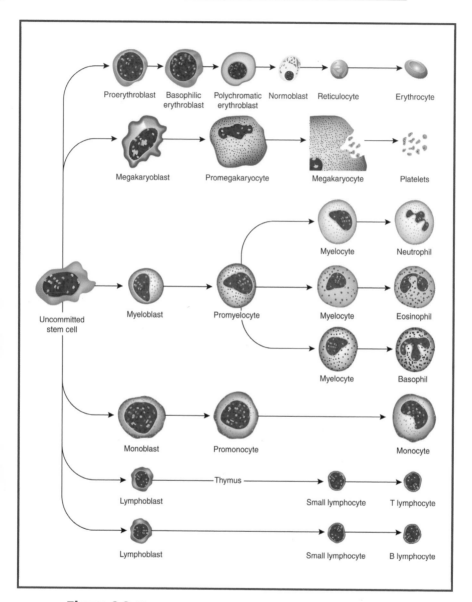

Figure 3.2 There are a variety of formed elements found in blood. All blood cells arise from stem cells located in the bone marrow. Note that during development, red blood cells lose many of their internal organelles. Mature red blood cells have a biconcave shape and are packed with hemoglobin molecules. Platelets are cell fragments that arise from megakaryocytes. The different cells that can form from an uncommitted stem cell are diagrammed here.

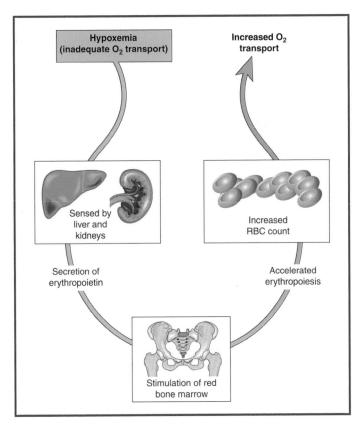

Figure 3.3 A decrease in the oxygen-carrying capacity of the blood is sensed by the liver and kidney, which, in turn, secrete the hormone erythropoietin. Erythropoietin stimulates the production of red blood cells in the bone marrow, returning the oxygen-carrying capacity of blood to normal. This process is illustrated here.

hematocrit can result from blood loss (injury or menstruation) and any condition causing anemia (low numbers of red blood cells). The hematocrit of males is higher than that of females because the male sex steroid, testosterone, stimulates erythropoietin synthesis by the kidney.

ABO Blood Type and the Rh Factor

There are four different ABO blood types in the general human population: A, B, AB, and O. These designations refer to whether an individual possesses specific proteins with or without certain polysaccharides, also known as **antigens**, on the surface of their red blood cells. An individual with type A blood has the A antigen on the surface of his/her red blood cells. Type B individuals have the B version of this antigen. Both the A and B antigens are present on the red blood cells of a person with type AB blood. Type O refers to the absence of both the A and B antigens (Figure 3.4). The absence of antigens on the red blood cells is noted by the word "negative," and the presence of antigens on the surface of the red blood cells is noted by the word "positive." Thus, an individual with O negative blood has neither A nor B antigens on their red blood cells, and an individual with AB positive blood has both A and B antigens of their red blood cells.

An individual with type A blood has antibodies against the B antigen. **Antibodies** are produced by the immune system to fight foreign invaders like viruses and bacteria. Antibodies help destroy these invaders by binding to the foreign antigens and triggering a series of events to destroy the foreign antigen-bearing invader. To a person with type A blood, type B blood is perceived as a foreign and potentially harmful invader. Antibodies will bind to the B antigen and initiate events that lead to destruction of the type B blood cells.

Figure 3.4 lists which donor blood types are compatible with the recipient's blood type in the event a blood transfusion is required. By examining the list of acceptable donor blood types, it is easy to understand why type O negative blood is in such high demand and why it is called the **universal donor blood type**— that is, O type blood has neither A antigens nor B antigens on the surface of its red blood cells. It also does not have Rh antigens. Type AB positive is considered to be the **universal recipient blood type**, in that an individual with Type AB positive blood can safely receive transfusions of all other blood types.

Rh (which stands for "Rhesus") factor represents a different type of antigen also located on the surface of the red blood cell. A person with Rh positive blood has the antigen. A person with Rh negative does not have the antigen. As with ABO blood

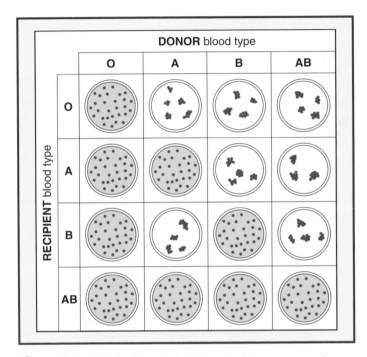

Figure 3.4 ABO blood type is determined by the presence or absence of the A and B antigens on the surface of an individual's red blood cells. An individual's blood type also determines what antibodies he or she carries. The diagram above shows which blood types are compatible. For example, when type A blood is given to a recipient who has type B blood, the blood cells clump together, demonstrating their incompatibility.

type, an individual who has Rh negative blood (i.e., has no Rh antigens on the surface of their red blood cells) will possess antibodies against the Rh factor. A person transfused with the wrong type blood may suffer a massive adverse immune reaction to the mismatched blood and could die.

White Blood Cells

Leukocytes, or **white blood cells**, are involved in helping the body defend itself against infection. The specific roles of the various types of leukocytes are addressed in the *Immune System* title of this series. Leukocytes are divided into two major groups: granulocytes, which have many granules, and agranulo-cytes, which have no granules. These cells are classified based on their staining patterns when viewed under a microscope.

Cells that when stained reveal a multilobed nucleus and the presence of many stained granules are called **polymorphonuclear granulocytes**. There are three types of granulocytes (refer again to Figure 3.2). **Neutrophils** are the most abundant type and play a significant role in the inflammatory process. **Eosinophils** fight against multicellular parasites and are involved in allergic reactions. **Basophils** contribute to the inflammatory process by releasing the chemical histamine.

There are two types of agranulocytes: lymphocytes and monocytes. **Lymphocytes** possess little cytoplasm around their large nuclei and are key to specific immu-nity, the ability of the human immune system to target specific disease-causing agents. **Monocytes**, large cells with oval-shaped nuclei and only a few granules, represent another class of leukocytes. Upon entering tissues, these cells transform into macrophages that can consume foreign cells or cellular debris and play a critical role in the destruction of infectious microorganisms.

Like red blood cells, all of these types of leukocytes are produced in the bone marrow, although some mature in organs such as the thymus gland.

Platelets

Platelets are small cell fragments that circulate in the blood in high numbers and promote clotting to reduce blood loss when blood vessels are damaged. Large cells in the bone marrow called **megakaryocytes** provide a constant source of these valuable cell fragments.

Platelets function in two key steps in the body's rapid response to stop bleeding. First, platelets form a plug at the wound site by sticking to the exposed collagen layer of the blood vessel (Figure 3.5). Once a few platelets bind, they become activated and release a variety of important chemicals.

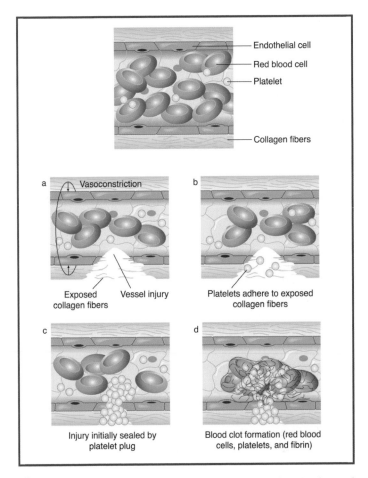

Figure 3.5 Clot formation at a break in the wall of a blood vessel is illustrated here. **Vasoconstriction**, or the reduction in the diameter of the vessel, reduces blood flow and blood loss. Platelets adhere to the damaged tissue, releasing chemoattractants that bring more platelets to the site. The plug formed as a result provides a temporary seal, allowing time for the blood vessel to repair the damage. The coagulation process generates the production of mesh-like fibers called **fibrin**.

Some of the chemicals stimulate more platelets to bind to the site so that a platelet plug is formed. Other chemicals stimulate the damaged vessel to contract, decreasing the flow of blood to the site of injury, thus slowing blood loss.

In addition to their role in rapidly forming a plug, platelets are also involved in the next phase of preventing blood loss, the **coagulation**, or blood-clotting, process. A blood clot forms around the platelet plug and helps to stabilize it. The plasma, or liquid portion of the blood, contains clotting factors (inactive forms of clotting enzymes). When certain clotting factors come into contact with the damaged area of the blood vessel, they become activated and trigger a cascade of events that lead to clot formation.

One of the key reactions involved in the clot formation cascade is the conversion of **prothrombin** to **thrombin**. Thrombin is the plasma enzyme that activates the formation of a mesh-like tangle of protein strands that form the structural scaffolding for the clot. These protein strands, called **fibrin**, are generated from the circulating protein fibrinogen in the presence of thrombin. Other plasma enzymes strengthen the fibrin network, which, once stabilized, begins to trap blood cells to complete the clot formation process.

Unfortunately, damage to the blood vessels can result from factors other than injury. **Atherosclerosis**, or the development of arterial plaques that can lead to heart disease, can cause damage to blood vessel walls. Exposure of the underlying vessel layers can trigger the clotting cascade, generating a blood clot that may block the vessel. If this clot formation occurs in a coronary artery, it may block blood (and hence oxygen) flow to the heart and cause a heart attack, a condition discussed in Chapter 5.

Many Americans have atherosclerosis, also called hardening of the arteries. Anticlotting drugs are frequently prescribed to reduce the risk of heart attack. One of the most commonly used drugs, aspirin, interferes with platelet aggregation, one of the early and key steps in triggering clot formation. Other anticlotting medications interfere with vitamin K production, a factor needed by the liver for the synthesis of clotting proteins. Certain drugs, called clot-busters, are used only after surgery or stroke to dissolve clots that have already formed. Clot-busters reduce the risk of stroke, a form of brain damage that occurs when a clot breaks free, lodges in a blood vessel in the brain, and disrupts the brain's oxygen supply.

Although the formation of blood clots in some individuals leads to dangerous conditions such as stroke and heart attack, others suffer from an inability to form blood clots. **Hemophilia** refers to several hereditary blood-clotting disorders involving a deficiency in one or more of the clotting factors. The coagulation process involves a cascade of reactions and several clotting factors. Because each clotting factor initiates the next reaction in the cascade, a deficiency in any one of these factors can reduce the amount of thrombin and fibrin produced.

The most common type of hemophilia, known as hemophilia A, involves a deficiency in a clotting factor called factor VIII. This genetic disorder affects one in 5,000 males and affected many of the male descendents of Queen Victoria of England. The defective gene is carried on the X chromosome and is, therefore, sex-linked. Recombinant DNA technology has led to large-scale production of the factor VIII protein and now helps to prevent the debilitating symptoms and death associated with the more severe cases of hemophilia A. Clotting factors that treat patients with other types of hemophilia are also now available through advances in this technology.

PLASMA

Plasma is the liquid, or extracellular portion, of blood tissue. As discussed in the previous section, plasma contains proteins that are critical to the clotting process. In fact, to obtain plasma with its dissolved clotting proteins, it is necessary to include an anticoagulant, such as heparin, in the collection tube. If no anticoagulant is present in the tube, the blood will clot, removing clotting proteins such as fibrinogen. Plasma without its clotting proteins is called **serum.**

Plasma contains a variety of other dissolved substances in addition to clotting proteins. **Albumins** and **globulins** are two

ARTIFICIAL BLOOD

Every year in the United States, more than 23 million units of blood are given to patients. Many people donate blood to replenish the supplies in blood banks. There are, however, dangers and expenses associated with receiving donated blood. Many blood-borne diseases, such as HIV and hepatitis C, have been transmitted through blood transfusions. Donated blood must be carefully screened for such diseases before it can be used.

Donated blood must also be typed to prevent life-threatening reactions caused by a patient receiving an incompatible blood type. The universal donor blood type, O negative, is in high demand, but only 6.6% of the population possesses this blood type. Storing blood can be a problem as well, particularly under military and other field conditions. Donated blood has a limited shelf life and must be discarded after six weeks.

Because modern medicine relies on a continuous supply of donated blood, scientists have been working to develop a blood substitute. One of the more promising solutions involves the development of artificial hemoglobin, the oxygen transport molecule, through genetic-engineering technology. A cell-free hemoglobin transfusion solution would avoid the need for blood typing and screening and would simplify storage requirements. Genetic modifications allow artificial hemoglobin to function like natural hemoglobin outside the specialized environment normally provided by the red blood cell. Unprotected hemoglobin is rapidly destroyed, and transfusions of hemoglobin would need to be given repeatedly. In addition, cell-free hemoglobin solutions appear to trigger high blood pressure in some patients by stimu-lating constriction of the blood vessels.

Other groups of scientists are attempting to develop an artificial red blood cell using pig blood. This option has some advantages over the cell-free system in that the hemoglobin is protected within a cell and does not degrade as quickly or increase blood pressure. However, the risk of disease transmission increases with the use of pig blood. Although these and other substitutes have been developed, as of yet, none are as safe or effective as donated blood. Scientists predict it will be years before a safe alternative is available.

additional classes of plasma proteins that serve a variety of important functions in the blood. For example, they help to maintain blood volume. Moreover, several of these proteins are involved in the transport of other substances, particularly hydrophobic molecules such as steroid hormones that do not dissolve well in plasma. Some of the globulins represent antibodies, proteins that are required for immunity against disease.

A variety of hormones can be detected in the plasma either directly dissolved in the fluid or bound to transport proteins. A plasma sample can also provide levels of key electrolytes, gases, and nutrients. In Chapter 5, you will learn how blood and its precious cargo is circulated throughout the body.

CONNECTIONS

Blood is a connective tissue consisting of cells and cell fragments suspended in an extracellular fluid matrix called plasma. Red blood cells constitute about 45% of the volume of whole blood. Their biconcave shape provides a large surface area for oxygen diffusion. These cells are packed with hemoglobin, the respiratory protein that binds and transports oxygen to the respiring tissues. White blood cells fight infection, and platelets function in blood clotting. All blood cells originate from stem cells in the bone marrow.

Blood transports many substances throughout the body, such as oxygen, nutrients, hormones, and cellular waste. It transports oxygen from the lungs and nutrients from the digestive system and other organs to the tissues. Hormones are chemical messenger molecules that are transported to their target tissues by the blood. Blood removes cellular waste products for elimination. It distributes heat, water, and electrolytes throughout the body. It is no wonder that we are often asked to provide a blood sample. No other bodily tissue can provide such a diversity of information about our health.

4

Oxygen Transport: The Role of Hemoglobin

In the last chapter, you learned that red blood cells are stripped-down cells packed with the respiratory protein hemoglobin. This chapter will focus on the structure and function of this important transport protein. Hemoglobin and a related protein called myoglobin bind oxygen and were the first proteins to be intensively studied by biochemists. As a result, the relationship between their structure and function is well understood.

The amount of oxygen that can be directly dissolved in blood is very small. Only 3 milliliters (ml) of oxygen can be dissolved in 1 liter (L) of blood. The amount of oxygen is limited by the fact that oxygen is not very soluble in water or blood and by the amount of oxygen available in the atmosphere. More than 98% of the oxygen in the blood is bound to hemoglobin molecules.

THE STRUCTURE OF HEMOGLOBIN
Each red blood cell is estimated to hold about 280 million hemoglobin molecules. **Hemoglobin** is composed of a protein component, called **globin**, and a pigment component, called **heme**. Each globin consists of four separate polypeptide chains that are bound together. Each chain has a heme group attached to it (Figure 4.1). Two of the polypeptide chains consist of identical

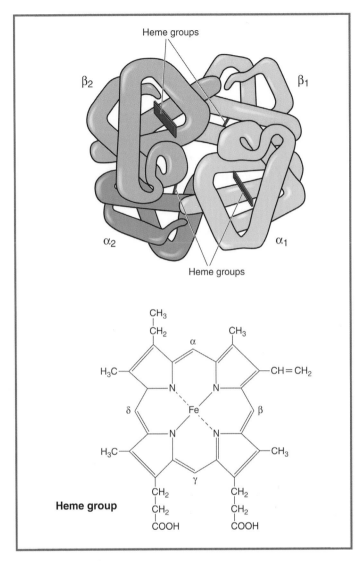

Figure 4.1 Hemoglobin, the structure of which is shown here, consists of four polypeptide chains, two alpha (α) and two beta (β) chains, with one heme group bound at each center. The heme groups have an iron atom, Fe^{2+}, to which a molecule of oxygen can bind. Hence, each hemoglobin molecule can bind four oxygen molecules.

alpha chains and two chains are identical beta chains. The chains are held together by chemical bonds to stabilize the hemoglobin structure.

Two different genes code for these globin proteins, one gene for the alpha chain and another for the beta chain. The hemoglobin of human fetuses contains an alternate globin gene. Instead of two alpha and two beta chains, fetal hemoglobin contains two alpha and two gamma chains. As a result, fetal hemoglobin binds oxygen more tightly than adult hemoglobin does. This important property of fetal blood allows for the transfer of oxygen from maternal to fetal hemoglobin within the placenta.

Another variant of human globin genes occurs with sickle-cell disease, also known as sickle-cell anemia. In this hereditary disorder, a substitution of one of the amino acids in the beta chain, which is 146 amino acids in length, leads to a variety of symptoms, some of which can be very debilitating (see box on page 41).

At the center of each heme group is an iron (Fe^{2+}) atom to which a single oxygen molecule can bind.

HEMOGLOBIN AND THE COOPERATIVE BINDING OF OXYGEN

The term **affinity** is used to describe hemoglobin's ability to bind oxygen. The binding of one oxygen molecule to one of the heme groups results in a slight shape, or conformational, change in the globin component. This slight change in the structure of the globin chain is transmitted to the remaining three chains, increasing their affinity for oxygen. In other words, the binding of one oxygen molecule makes it easier to bind the next three oxygen molecules, a characteristic known as **cooperative binding**.

The relationship of cooperative binding to oxygen binding can best be described by examining a **saturation curve** for hemoglobin (Figure 4.2). A saturation curve compares the availability of oxygen in the surrounding environment with the degree, in percent, that the hemoglobin molecules are saturated with oxygen. For example, a saturation of

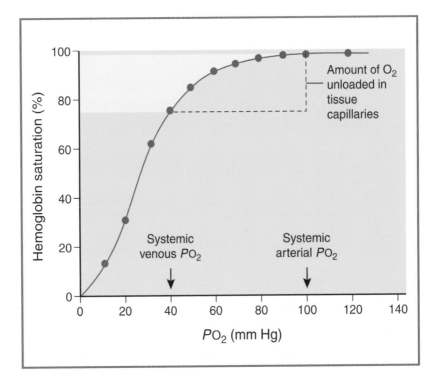

Figure 4.2 This is a typical oxygen saturation curve for hemoglobin. Note the sigmoidal, or S, shape of the curve, which is due to the cooperative binding of oxygen. Resting partial pressure (P) values for the lungs and systemic tissues are indicated on the graph. Typically, at rest, only 25% of the oxygen bound to hemoglobin is released to the tissues. The remaining 75% represents a circulating oxygen reserve.

100% would indicate that the hemoglobin molecules are fully saturated with oxygen (i.e., all four heme groups have oxygen molecules bound to them). Hemoglobin with no bound oxygen, also known as **deoxyhemoglobin**, is 0% saturated. If, on average, one of four sites on the hemoglobin molecules is occupied with oxygen, this hemoglobin solution would be 25% saturated.

Oxygen availability is measured by physiologists using units of pressure. In Figure 4.2 and in this book, we use millimeters of mercury (or mm Hg) as the units for pressure. The pressure of oxygen in the atmosphere or in a solution is expressed as a partial pressure (since it is not the only gas present). For this reason, the symbol for the partial pressure of oxygen is PO_2. At sea level, the PO_2 of the atmosphere is about 160 mm Hg. The PO_2 of the air within the human lung is about 100 mm Hg.

If there was no cooperative binding effect, a linear relationship between the amount of oxygen available in the environment (the PO_2) and the amount of O_2 bound to hemoglobin, or the percent saturation, would be expected. Instead, once the degree of saturation reaches 25%, small changes in oxygen availability result in greater amounts of oxygen bound.

For example, if the starting PO_2 level is 10 mm Hg, an increase in PO_2 of 10 mm Hg results in an increase of about 15% saturation (from 15 to 30%). If, however, the starting PO_2 is 20 mm Hg, an increase of 10 mm Hg results in an increase of about 30 percent saturation (from 30 to 60%). Within a certain range, small changes in oxygen availability result in relatively large changes in the oxygen saturation of hemoglobin.

To summarize, the ability of hemoglobin to bind oxygen, or its affinity for oxygen, increases when one oxygen molecule has bound to one of the heme groups. This enhanced ability to bind oxygen is caused by a conformational change in the globin, or protein, component of hemoglobin. This property of hemoglobin, called cooperative binding, is responsible for the S-shaped saturation curve.

THE TRANSPORT OF OXYGEN BY HEMOGLOBIN

In a healthy human at rest, the typical PO_2 levels, or oxygen concentrations, encountered by hemoglobin as it travels through the bloodstream are highest in the lungs, where oxygen is taken up from the atmosphere. The PO_2 of the blood leaving the lungs is typically 100 mm Hg at sea level. The lowest PO_2

SICKLE-CELL DISEASE

Sickle-cell disease, or sickle-cell anemia, was the first genetic disorder to be understood at the molecular level. As early as 1949, scientists observed the hemoglobin molecules of healthy individuals differed from those of sickle-cell patients. Later, it was determined that the mutation that causes this disease resides in the gene (called the sickling gene) that codes for the beta chain of the globin component of hemoglobin. A difference in a single DNA nucleotide results in the substitution of the amino acid glutamic acid for valine, altering just one of the 146 amino acids that compose the beta chain.

The sickling gene results in hemoglobin that crystallizes at low oxygen concentrations, deforming the typical biconcave shape of the red blood cell into a sickle-shaped form (Figure 4.3). The deformed red blood cells become lodged in the tiny capillaries, obstructing blood flow and oxygen delivery to tissues and causing pain and organ damage. A sickling crisis can be triggered in individuals with sickle-cell disease when the oxygen level of their blood is low, for example, at high altitude or with increased physical activity. Deformed red blood cells are removed from circulation and destroyed by the liver, resulting in a decreased number of circulating red blood cells, otherwise known as anemia.

Sickle-cell disease is an example of incomplete dominance, a form of inheritance in which an intermediate form of the trait is observed. In the case of incomplete dominance, a person who is heterozygous (i.e., has one healthy version of the gene and one sickling version) is usually healthy, but a percentage of people have some symptoms of the disease when experiencing a reduction of blood oxygen.

Sickle-cell disease is also of interest to evolutionary biologists. Malaria is a devastating disease that ravages many tropical regions of the world. It is caused by the parasite *Plasmodium falciparum*, which is carried by the *Anopheles gambiae* mosquito. The mosquito transmits the parasite to the humans it bites. Once in the bloodstream, the malarial parasite enters the red blood cells and is transported throughout the body.

The British geneticist Anthony Allison observed that the regions of Africa where the malarial parasite was most prevalent coincided with the regions where a large percentage of the human population was heterozygous for the sickling gene. It appears that the sickling gene protects against malarial infection. Those populations with a higher frequency of the trait tend to have milder, less devastating cases of malaria. The sickling gene and its effect on red blood cells render these cells uninhabitable by the malarial parasite, significantly reducing the degree of infection.

With information on the human genome and the genomes of *Plasmodium falciparum* and *Anopheles gambiae*, scientists hope to identify an effective means of reducing malaria's debilitating effect on human populations.

Figure 4.3 A mutation in the gene coding for the beta chain of the globin component of hemoglobin results in the deformation of the red blood cell. The typical biconcave shape of a red blood cell is shown on the left. The sickle shape of a red blood cell in people who have sickle-cell disease is shown on the right.

levels encountered by hemoglobin are in the tissues, where oxygen is consumed during the process of cellular respiration. The most metabolically active tissues, such as the kidneys and heart, will consume the most oxygen and as a consequence will have the lowest PO_2 levels. On average, however, tissue PO_2 levels are about 40 mm Hg.

Therefore, in a resting healthy human at sea level, circulating hemoglobin is traveling through PO_2 environments that vary from 40 to 100 mm Hg. To determine the degree to which hemoglobin is saturated with oxygen at both of these pressures (Figure 4.4a), it is necessary to examine the oxygen saturation curve. Hemoglobin entering the lungs from the tissues, where PO_2 levels are 40 mm Hg, will be 75% saturated with oxygen; thus, on average, three out of the four binding sites are occupied with oxygen molecules. Upon reaching the lungs, where the PO_2 levels are 100 mm Hg, the hemoglobin molecules become fully saturated with oxygen.

As these saturated hemoglobin molecules travel to the respiring tissues, where the PO_2 levels are 40 mm Hg, some of the oxygen is unloaded (about 25%) and the remaining 75% stays bound to hemoglobin. This remaining oxygen serves as an oxygen reserve within the blood for when an individual becomes more active and the rate of cellular respiration increases.

For example, when an individual begins to run, the leg muscles, heart, and respiratory muscles go from a resting state to a more active state. Because the rate of muscular contraction in these organs increases with running, the rates of cellular respiration must increase to provide adequate amounts of ATP, the form of energy required to fuel this activity. More oxygen will be needed for the process of cellular respiration. As more oxygen is consumed in these active tissues, their PO_2 levels begin to drop below 40 mm Hg. Let's observe what happens to the oxygen reserve in hemoglobin when it encounters these lower PO_2 environments (Figure 4.4b).

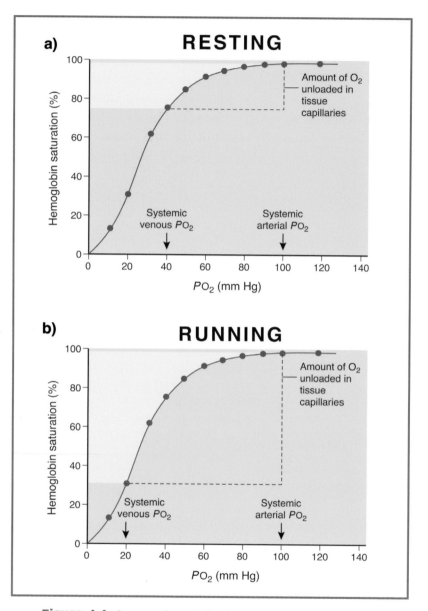

Figure 4.4 A comparison of the degree of oxygen saturation of hemoglobin in an individual at rest (a) and while running (b) is shown here. As the partial pressure of oxygen of the surrounding tissues drops, as shown in b, significantly more oxygen is released by hemoglobin, illustrating the use of the oxygen reserve.

If, for example, the PO_2 levels in certain leg muscles drop from the resting level of 40 mm Hg to 20 mm Hg with activity, hemoglobin encountering a PO_2 of 20 mm Hg will unload 70% of its oxygen, in contrast to 25% seen in the previous example. If we compare the two conditions with respect to the degree of saturation of hemoglobin, we can begin to appreciate the physiological importance of the S-shaped saturation curve. When hemoglobin that is fully saturated encounters a tissue PO_2 of 40 mm Hg, a change of 100–40 or 60 mm Hg, it unloads only 25% of its oxygen. However, when hemoglobin encounters a tissue PO_2 level of 20 mm Hg, a change of 100–20 or 80 mm Hg, it unloads fully 70% of the oxygen that it carries.

Below 40 mm Hg (the PO_2 of tissues at rest) small changes in tissue PO_2 levels result in greater amounts of oxygen released by hemoglobin. Hemoglobin is most responsive to the needs of active tissues. The circulating oxygen reserve can be readily tapped when needed. You should also be able to envision how hemoglobin traveling to a metabolically active tissue, like a contracting muscle, will lose more oxygen to that tissue. If, however, that same molecule had happened to circulate to a less active tissue, in part of the digestive system of someone who is running, less oxygen would have been released and the hemoglobin molecule would return to the lungs at a higher degree of saturation.

HEMOGLOBIN AND THE BOHR EFFECT

The unique S-shaped saturation curve is not the only characteristic of hemoglobin that contributes to its ability to release more oxygen to metabolically active tissues. In addition to responding to changing PO_2 levels, hemoglobin responds to the presence of other tissue factors that reflect the level of metabolic activity. As the rate of cellular respiration (Figure 4.5) increases, as seen with increased metabolic activity, the rate of oxygen consumed increases, causing PO_2 levels to

$$C_6H_{12}O_6 \text{ (fuel)} + 6O_2 \longrightarrow 6CO_2 + 6H_2O + ATP + Heat$$

Figure 4.5 The overall chemical reaction representing cellular respiration involves combining fuel and oxygen to produce carbon dioxide, water, ATP (energy), and heat. As the rate of cellular respiration increases, the rate at which oxygen is consumed increases. In addition, the amount of carbon dioxide and heat produced increases.

drop. In addition, as the rate of cellular respiration increases, the amount of CO_2, a waste product of cellular respiration, also increases. To summarize, increased cellular activity results in increased O_2 consumption and decreased PO_2 levels, as well as increased PCO_2 levels due to increased production of carbon dioxide.

The structure of hemoglobin is sensitive to PCO_2 levels. When circulating hemoglobin encounters an environment where the PCO_2 levels are elevated, the CO_2 decreases hemoglobin's affinity for oxygen and oxygen is released to the tissue. CO_2 reduces hemoglobin's ability to bind O_2 in two different ways, directly and indirectly. CO_2 can bind directly to the amino-terminal ends of the alpha and beta chains that make up the globin. The binding of CO_2 to hemoglobin causes a conformational change, reducing hemoglobin's hold on oxygen and, as a consequence, oxygen is released. The sensitivity of hemoglobin to PCO_2 levels can be illustrated on a saturation curve (Figure 4.6). The curve on the right, with a PCO_2 level of 40 mm Hg, represents carbon dioxide concentrations hemoglobin might encounter in the lungs. The curve on the left represents the PCO_2 levels that a hemoglobin molecule might encounter in the respiring tissues. You can see that the saturation curve for

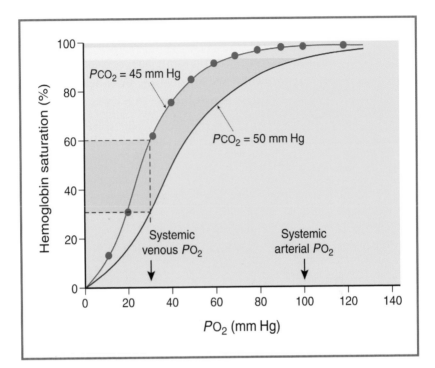

Figure 4.6 An increase in the partial pressure of carbon dioxide of the surrounding tissues results in a shift to the right of the oxygen saturation curve, indicating a decrease in hemoglobin's affinity for oxygen.

hemoglobin shifts to the right as higher and higher PCO_2 levels are encountered, a phenomenon called the **Bohr effect**.

A shift to the right of the oxygen saturation curve represents a decrease in the affinity of hemoglobin for oxygen. What is the physiological significance of this shift? Whenever you are trying to assess the consequences of any shift in the saturation curve for hemoglobin, it is best to start by choosing one PO_2 level for comparison. For this example, let's compare two saturation curves at a PO_2 of 30 mm Hg. Using the saturation curve at a PCO_2 of 45 mm Hg, a typical resting value of a respiring tissue, we can determine that hemoglobin encountering a PO_2 of 30 mm Hg will unload 40% of the oxygen it carries, i.e., it will remain 60% saturated with oxygen. However, if it encounters a higher PCO_2 of 50 mm Hg, it unloads even more oxygen, 70%, such that only 30% remains. More oxygen is released to environments with higher PCO_2 levels. In this way, hemoglobin is responsive to the PO_2 levels as well as the PCO_2 levels of the tissue it is circulating through.

Indirectly, higher PCO_2 levels have a similar effect through a change in the pH or acidity of the environment. The important relationship between CO_2 and pH levels can be best illustrated through a chemical reaction (Figure 4.7). As the amount of CO_2 rises, the concentration of H^+ increases and the pH drops (i.e., the environment becomes more acidic). The increased acidity also results in a shift to the right of the oxygen saturation curve as the affinity of hemoglobin for oxygen is reduced. Likewise, an increase in temperature of the surrounding environment also reduces hemoglobin's oxygen affinity, shifting the curve to the right.

To summarize, increased CO_2 levels, decreased pH (or increased acidity), and increased temperature are all factors that result in a decrease in hemoglobin's affinity for oxygen, thereby promoting oxygen release to the tissues. This is advantageous, since an increase in the rate of cellular respiration produces more CO_2, hence more H^+, and more heat.

CONNECTIONS

Hemoglobin, found in red blood cells, is the respiratory pigment that binds and transports oxygen in the blood. Its protein component consists of four polypeptide chains, two alpha and two beta chains, held together by chemical bonds. Each polypeptide chain has a heme molecule with a binding site for oxygen at its Fe^{2+} (iron) center. Therefore, each hemoglobin molecule can bind four oxygen molecules.

The binding of one molecule increases the affinity of hemoglobin for oxygen, making it easier to bind the next three oxygen molecules, a phenomenon known as cooperativity. As

$$CO_2 + H_2O \longrightarrow H_2CO_3 \longrightarrow HCO_3^- + H^+$$
(Carbon Dioxide + Water $\Rightarrow$ Carbonic Acid $\Rightarrow$ Bicarbonate + Hydrogen Ion)

Figure 4.7 The relationship between carbon dioxide levels and acidity can be seen in this chemical equation. An increase in carbon-dioxide levels causes an increase in hydrogen-ion concentration (H^+), increasing acidity and reducing the pH.

a result, hemoglobin's saturation curve is S-shaped and the affinity of hemoglobin for oxygen changes with the PO_2 of the surrounding environment.

Increased metabolic activity (i.e., an increased rate of cellular respiration) results in an increase in carbon-dioxide production, an increased acidity (or decrease in pH), and an increased temperature. Such changes will reduce the affinity of hemoglobin for oxygen, causing a shift to the right of its oxygen-saturation curve, and increase the amount of oxygen released to the tissues.

5

Anatomy of the Circulatory System

As described in **Chapter 2, the human circulatory system is divided** into two separate circuits, the systemic circuit and the pulmonary circuit (Figure 5.1). Each of these circuits consists of a similar sequence of blood vessels. Blood is pumped out of the heart into arteries of decreasing size that merge into arterioles before reaching the sites of exchange with the capillaries. Blood leaving the capillaries is gathered into venules and then veins before returning to the heart. The systemic circuit, the left side of the heart, provides the pressure to propel blood to the entire body. The pulmonary circuit, the right side of the heart, takes blood to the lungs for gas exchange with the atmosphere.

In this chapter, you will examine the anatomy of the heart and blood vessels. You will also learn about two common circulatory diseases afflicting millions of Americans, atherosclerosis and **myocardial infarction (heart attack**).

ANATOMY OF THE HEART

The heart beats steadily from early in embryonic development until death. If a person lives until 75 years of age, and during that time his or her heart beats an average of 75 times per minute, by the time the person dies, the heart will have beat a total of 3 billion times and pumped more than 200 million liters of blood.

The heart is located in the chest, or thoracic, cavity with the lungs. It lies slightly left of the midline of the body. Because the heart takes

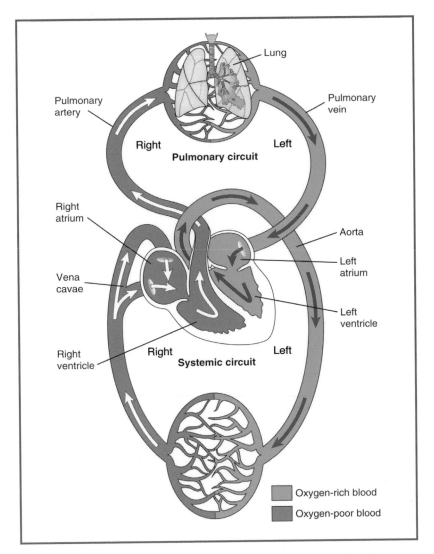

Figure 5.1 An overview of the pulmonary and systemic circuits of the human circulatory system is illustrated here. The human heart has four chambers. The right atrium and ventricle pump blood into the pulmonary circuit, while the left atrium and ventricle move blood into the systemic circuit. For both circuits, blood leaving the heart travels through arteries, then the arterioles, and the capillaries. In the pulmonary circuit, gas exchange occurs in the capillaries in the lungs. In the systemic circuit, gas exchange occurs with the bodily tissues. Blood leaving the capillaries is gathered into venules and then veins before returning to the heart. In this diagram, blue blood represents blood of low oxygen content, and the red blood represents fully oxygenated blood.

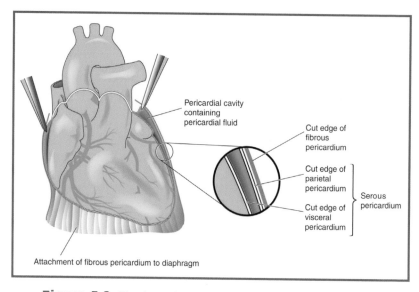

Pericardial cavity
containing
pericardial fluid

Cut edge of
fibrous
pericardium

Cut edge of
parietal
pericardium

Serous
pericardium

Cut edge of
visceral
pericardium

Attachment of fibrous pericardium to diaphragm

Figure 5.2 The heart is surrounded by the pericardium, two layers of membrane separated by pericardial fluid. The fluid helps lubricate the heart and reduce friction. The tough outer membrane of the pericardium (fibrous pericardium) helps keep the heart in place during its vigorous beating actions.

up more space on the left side of the chest cavity, the left lung has two lobes, compared to the three lobes of the right lung. The heart is surrounded by a pericardium, a lining that separates the heart from the lungs and the chest wall (Figure 5.2). The pericardium consists of two membranes with fluid between them—the fibrous portion and the serous portion. This pericardial fluid lubricates the heart and reduces friction during beating. The tough outer pericardial membrane (fibrous pericardium) lines the outer surface of the heart and helps keep the heart in position while beating.

The heart possesses four chambers, two **atria** (plural for **atrium**) and two **ventricles** (Figure 5.3). The right side of the heart, consisting of the right atrium and right ventricle, is separated from the left side of the heart by a wall, or septum. The right and left side of the heart may beat as one unit, but

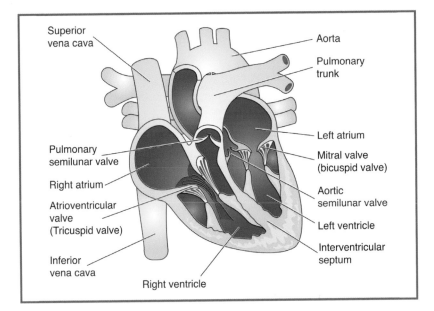

Figure 5.3 The basic anatomy of the human heart includes the chambers, known as atria and ventricles, the attached major blood vessels, and the two types of heart valves, the semilunar and atrioventricular valves. Recall that the right side of the heart sends blood to the lungs, and the left side supplies the entire body. Note the thickness of the left ventricular wall.

they are completely separate from each other with respect to the blood they contain. Both the right and left atria are separated from their respective ventricles by the **atrioventricular (AV) valves,** folds of tough tissue that open in one direction only, from the atrium into the ventricle. Atrioventricular valves are also known as cuspid valves.

The atria receive blood returning to the heart and then pump that blood into the ventricles. The ventricles are the more muscular pumps of the heart, because they must generate enough force to propel the blood out into circulation against the pressures existing in the two circuits. The muscular walls of the atria are thinner than those of the ventricles, reflecting the fact that they do not have to generate the high forces required of the ventricles. Similarly, because the left ventricle must generate enough force to overcome the higher pressure existing in the systemic circuit and propel blood for longer distances, its muscular walls are thicker than those of the right ventricle. The right ventricle supplies the pulmonary circuit, where the distance traveled by the blood is short and blood pressure is lower.

The primary component of both the atrial and ventricular walls is **cardiac muscle**. Although all muscle tissue is specialized for contraction, cardiac muscle has some characteristics that differ from the skeletal muscle used to move the joints, reflecting its unique function. For example, individual cardiac muscle cells are smaller than skeletal muscle cells, and they contain a single nucleus (Figure 5.4). Cardiac muscle cells are well-connected to each other through regions known as **intercalated discs**. A high density of adhesion molecules known as **desmosomes** keep the cells tightly attached to each other in these regions, ensuring that the forces generated during the beating actions of the heart do not rip apart the heart muscle. **Gap junctions** allow ions to move from one cardiac cell to another, and, as you will learn in Chapter 6, these junctions help the heart muscle to synchronize its actions.

The muscular walls of the atria are easily stretched and can accommodate large volumes of blood returning to the heart. The right atrium receives blood returning from the systemic circuit via two large veins, the **superior vena cava**, which drains all regions above the heart, and the **inferior vena cava**, which collects blood returning from the lower body regions (refer again to Figure 5.3). The AV valve separating the right atrium and ventricle is sometimes called the **tricuspid valve** because it is composed of three flaps of tissue. This valve opens only when blood pressure in the atria exceeds ventricular pressure, thus preventing any backflow into the atria when the pressure gradient is reversed. The left AV valve, or **bicuspid valve**, serves a similar function between the left atrium and ventricle, but consists of two flaps instead of three.

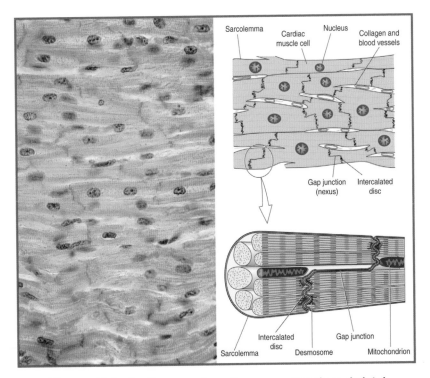

Figure 5.4 Cardiac muscle cells are smaller than skeletal muscle cells and are connected through structures known as intercalated discs. Desmosomes, or adhesion molecules, help to hold the cardiac cells together during contractions. Gap junctions allow for synchronization of heart contractions. A photograph of actual cardiac muscle is shown on the left. The illustrations on the right depict the components of cardiac muscle.

The cone-shaped left and right ventricles are similar in design. The right ventricle pushes blood out into the pulmonary circuit through a **pulmonary semilunar valve**, which separates the ventricular chamber from the pulmonary trunk. This valve opens when ventricular pressure exceeds pulmonary trunk pressure, otherwise it remains closed. In a similar fashion, the **aortic semilunar valve** separates the left ventricle from the **ascending aorta**. Both semilunar valves prevent blood from flowing back into the heart once it has had been forced out into circulation.

The importance of the AV and semilunar valves is under-scored by conditions that lead to their malfunction. Rheumatic fever, a condition that may develop after an infection with *Streptococcus*, can lead to valve dysfunction even decades after the infection occurred. Some individuals are born with malformations of their heart valves. Regardless of the cause, malfunctioning valves can cause debilitating reductions in cardiac function. Surgical repair and replacement, often with valves obtained from the similar-sized pig heart, is a common treatment for these valvular diseases.

CORONARY-ARTERY DISEASE AND HEART ATTACK

Coronary arteries bring oxygen-rich blood to the hardworking heart muscle. The blockage of these arteries, as well as others in the body, most often arises from a condition known as atherosclerosis. With this disease, calcified fatty deposits build up to form so-called plaques in the inner lining of these arteries. If these plaques grow large enough to reduce blood flow, the heart's access to oxygen and nutrients may be affected and its ability to function impaired. If a plaque ruptures, the blood clot that forms as a result may block the artery completely or break free and lodge in another smaller artery. In either of these cases, if the flow of blood to a region of the heart is interrupted for more than a few minutes, permanent damage to that region in the form of a myocardial infarction (better known as a heart attack) is very likely to occur. The extent and severity of the damage determines whether the individual who suffered the attack will live or die. Warning signs of an impending heart attack may include **angina**, or chest pain. People suffering from angina often experience the pain when they exert them-selves. As their level of activity increases, the heart works harder to compensate and is more likely to become oxygen-deprived.

THE CORONARY ARTERIES

The heart is a hardworking muscle and therefore needs an ample supply of oxygen and fuel. The heart muscle does not gain these essentials from the blood it is pumping; instead, it requires its own extensive blood supply. The **coronary arteries** serve this function. Recall that the left ventricle pumps blood out into the systemic circuit, through the left semilunar valve, and into the ascending aorta. At the base of the ascending aorta, the right and left coronary arteries branch off to bring oxygen-rich blood to

The risk factors associated with atherosclerosis include high levels of "bad" cholesterol, or LDL, and low levels of HDL, or "good" cholesterol. There is increased incidence for older individuals, for people with high blood pressure or diabetes, and for those who smoke, are obese, or are inactive. Genetics also appears to play a role. Medical practitioners use blood tests, ECGs (electrocardiograms), stress tests, and techniques that visualize the blood flow through the coronary or other arteries to diagnose the presence of atherosclerosis.

Clogged coronary arteries can be opened using **angioplasty**. Plaques can be removed or pressed into the arterial wall using an inflated balloon. If these procedures fail to increase blood flow to the heart muscle adequately, then coronary bypass surgery may be performed. For this treatment, small vessels, like the great saphenous vein of the leg, are removed to replace a diseased section of a coronary artery. A quadruple bypass surgery means that four separate coronary arteries are bypassed using this technique during one operation. Bypass surgery has become safer and fairly routine and is successful at improving heart function and reducing angina in most individuals with coronary-artery disease.

their respective sides of the heart. Blood flow through these arteries can increase up to nine times the resting rate during intensive exercise, when the heart is pumping maximally. The coronary arteries of a large number of Americans are diseased, reducing the ability of their hearts to function properly (see box on page 56).

THE BLOOD VESSELS

The circulatory system consists of the heart, the blood vessels, and blood. We have just examined the structure and function of the heart, the muscular pump that provides the force to circulate blood throughout the body. Previously, we discussed the composition of blood, the fluid medium that transports oxygen, nutrients, and water to our cells and removes wastes. Now, we will examine the types of blood vessels found in the human circulatory system.

Within each of the two circuits, there are five basic types of blood vessels: arteries, arterioles, capillaries, venules, and veins. Each type of blood vessel differs in form and function.

When blood is first ejected from the heart, it enters large **arteries** that immediately begin to branch into medium-sized and then smaller arteries. The arteries receive the pressurized blood from the heart and distribute it to all of the body's tissues, including the heart itself. Arterial walls are thick because they are very muscular. The larger arteries have elastic walls that can withstand the enormous changes in blood pressure that accompany the actions of the heart. These vessels are designed for efficiently transporting blood away from the heart.

The medium-sized arteries distribute blood to the skeletal muscles and major organs. These arteries, in general, have a thinner layer of muscle, although the difference in structure from the larger arteries is subtle. Overall, the diameters of the vessels decrease and proportion of the muscle of the arterial wall decreases as the arteries become smaller.

Arterioles are small arteries that have an inner layer of smooth muscle cells. These vessels play the more critical role in determining blood pressure. If the arterioles receive a signal to **vasodilate**, or increase their diameter, blood pressure is reduced. Conversely, when stimulated to decrease their diameter, or **vasoconstrict**, they can initiate a profound increase in an individual's blood pressure. For this reason, the arterioles are called the **resistance vessels**. When they are vasoconstricted, they resist blood flow and increase blood pressure.

Arterioles connect to capillaries, the sites for exchange between the blood and the tissues. Fick's law of diffusion dictates that capillary walls should be thin to minimize the diffusion distance and maximize the exchange rate, and this is indeed the case. The typical capillary wall consists only of a single layer of endothelium surrounded by a thin basement membrane. The diameter of these vessels is so small that red blood cells can barely squeeze through single file. The rate of blood flow through the capillaries is quite slow, permitting ample time for exchange with the tissues.

Capillaries are organized into interconnected units called **capillary beds**. Blood may be restricted from entering a capillary bed if rings of smooth muscle, or **precapillary sphincters**, are constricted. When the sphincters are relaxed, blood flows into the bed. In this way, blood flow to a specific region can be adjusted based on the need for oxygen. How this change in flow to a region is regulated will be discussed in Chapter 7. The precapillary sphincters typically exhibit cycles of relaxation (opening) and constriction (closing) such that blood flow through capillary beds is pulsatile (on and off), exhibiting a pattern known as **vasomotion**.

Capillaries empty into **venules**, small-diameter veins. The venules merge into medium-sized veins, which then merge into larger-diameter veins. Veins return blood to the heart and differ in a number of ways from arteries. For example, the walls of veins are thinner and the lumens are larger, characteristics that render veins collapsible. Veins serve as **capacitance vessels** for the circulatory system, holding up to 65% of the body's entire blood volume at any one time.

In addition, large veins have valves that keep blood flowing in the direction of the heart (Figure 5.5). These valves work in a fashion similar to the heart valves, that is, they only allow blood to flow in one direction. When the blood pressure is greater below the valve, the valve is forced open and the blood moves closer to the heart. This change in pressure could happen, for example, when a leg muscle contracts and squeezes down on the vein. When blood pressure on both sides of the valve is equal, or if it is greater above the valve, the valve remains closed, so blood can never flow away from the heart, despite a pressure gradient that might favor such backflow.

The presence of these valves is especially important in the large leg veins of a standing person. The blood returning to the heart is under very low pressure and is moving against the force of gravity. The valves will help prevent blood from pooling in the lower extremities under such circumstances, although periodic contractions of the skeletal muscles are required to squeeze down on the veins to push the blood past the valves.

CONNECTIONS

The heart is a powerful muscle that is divided into four blood-filled chambers: two atria and two ventricles. Valves separate the atria from the ventricles, and the ventricles from the blood vessels they supply, ensuring that blood flows through the heart in only one direction. The right side of the heart pumps blood through the pulmonary circuit, where it becomes oxygenated in the pulmonary capillaries. The oxygenated blood is then returned to the left side of the heart and pumped out into the systemic circuit.

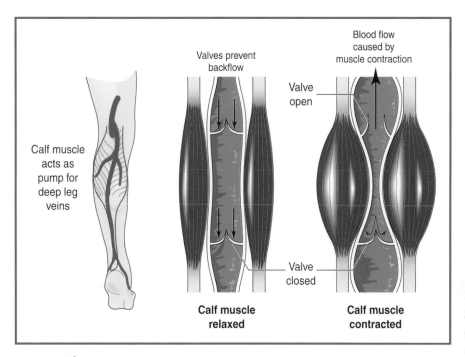

Figure 5.5 Blood pressures in the venous system are much lower than those in the arterial system. The larger veins possess valves that promote the return of blood to the heart. Contraction of the skeletal muscle surrounding a vein will squeeze the blood above the valve and prevent any backflow from occurring. This concept is illustrated here.

The heart beats constantly and requires an ample blood supply that is provided by the coronary arteries. Coronary-artery diseases, such as atherosclerosis, affect millions of Americans and put them at increased risk for heart attacks.

Blood leaving the heart courses through the arteries, arterioles, capillaries, venules, and, finally, the veins before returning to the heart. Each of these blood vessels possesses unique characteristics that support its function. Capillaries are organized into functional networks known as capillary beds and represent the site of gas exchange between the blood and the tissues.

6

Pumping Blood: How the Heart Works

In the last chapter, we learned how the heart is organized as an organ. It has four hollow chambers that fill with blood. Valves keep blood flowing in a single direction at all times through the heart and the remainder of the circulatory system. We also explored how the cardiac muscle cells are interconnected both physically, through the presence of strong adhesion molecules known as desmosomes, and functionally, through gap junctions.

In this chapter, you will learn how the heart generates the pressures necessary to propel blood through the pulmonary and systemic circuits. You will learn that the heart generates its own rhythm of beating, a rhythm that can be influenced by the nervous and endocrine systems. The heart pumps constantly and increases its efforts when necessary to accommodate changes in a person's activity level.

THE CONDUCTING SYSTEM OF THE HEART

Every time the heart beats, the atria and ventricles contract in coordination so that blood is forced out into circulation throughout the body. The cells responsible for initiating this coordinated contraction reside within the heart muscle itself (i.e., the heart generates its own rhythm). A specialized system of cells then relays this stimulus quickly

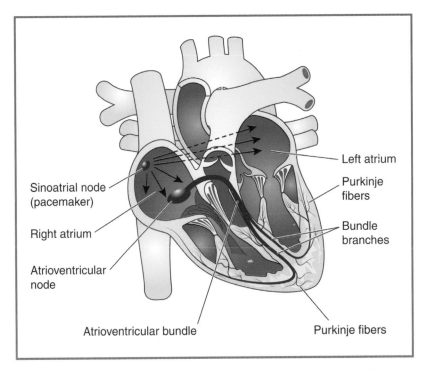

Sinoatrial node (pacemaker)

Right atrium

Atrioventricular node

Atrioventricular bundle

Left atrium

Purkinje fibers

Bundle branches

Purkinje fibers

Figure 6.1 The conducting system of the heart is important to the coordination of atrial and ventricular contractions. Pacemaker cells in the SA node of the right atrium generate a signal that is relayed to the AV node. From there, the signal is transmitted to the ventricles via the AV bundle, the bundle branches, and the Purkinje fibers.

throughout the heart muscle. This conducting system of the heart consists of the following tissues: the sinoatrial node, the atrioventricular node, the atrioventricular bundle, and the Purkinje fibers. There also are a number of conducting cells involved in relaying this signal between each of these tissues.

The **sinoatrial (SA) node** is located in the wall of the right atrium (Figure 6.1). Within this structure are **pacemaker cells** that generate the heart rate. Pacemaker cells are **autorhythmic**, that is, they generate their own rhythm that can then be altered by input from the nervous system. These cells do not maintain a stable resting state like most other cells do; instead, they spontaneously initiate an electrical impulse, which appears as a spike in a recording of pacemaker activity (Figure 6.2). This

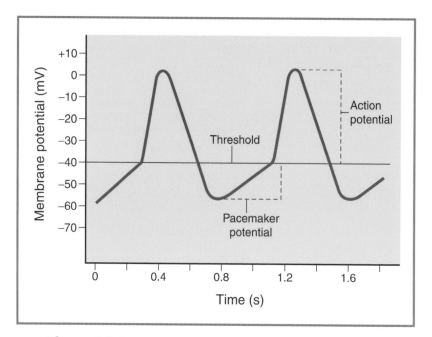

Figure 6.2 Pacemaker cells in the sinoatrial node of the right atrium do not remain in the resting state; instead, they spontaneously depolarize, moving the membrane potential toward threshold. Once the membrane potential reaches threshold, an excitatory signal is generated and then spread throughout the heart by the conducting system.

electrical impulse rapidly spreads to the other cells of the heart. After firing, the pacemaker cells rest for a brief period before generating a new wave of excitation.

This excitatory signal is rapidly relayed via conducting cells to the atrioventricular (AV) node, located at the base of the right atrium. At the same time, this signal is relayed throughout the right and left atrial muscle tissue and stimulates their contraction. The AV node slows the relay of the signal to the ventricles. This delay is critical to proper heart function. The atria need adequate time to contract down onto the volumes of blood within, force open the AV valves, and fill the ventricles before they begin to contract. Thus, the delay of the signal at the AV node ensures adequate filling of the ventricles. Because of this delay, the atria always contract before the ventricles, and while the ventricles are contracting, the atria are relaxing.

After the delay, the signal is then relayed from the AV node to the AV bundle located in the wall that separates the two ventricles. The AV bundle splits into two separate branches, one for each ventricle. As the branches reach the apex, or bottom tip, of the heart, they begin to branch into structures known as **Purkinje fibers.** The Purkinje fibers quickly spread the excitatory signal throughout the ventricular muscle tissue, stimulating contraction of the ventricles in a coordinated manner. Because the wave of contraction starts at the apex of the heart, blood is forced up and out of the semilunar valves and into the pulmonary and systemic circuits.

The coordination of atrial and ventricular contractions is necessary for efficient pumping of the blood. Any damage to the conducting system of heart leads to a loss of coordination and diminished heart function. Cardiac arrhymthmias, or abnormalities in the conducting pathway of the heart, can be detected using an **electrocardiogram**, or **ECG** (sometimes abbreviated as **EKG**). With this procedure, electrodes are placed on key points of the body surface to monitor the electrical activity of the heart.

Some of the more common features of an ECG recording are illustrated in Figure 6.3. The small **P wave** represents the spread of the excitatory signal throughout the atria. The **QRS complex** results from the ventricular depolarization, as the signal spreads via the AV bundle and the Purkinje fibers. The **T wave** results from the repolarization, or return to the resting state, of the ventricles. The QRS complex masks the corresponding wave representing atrial repolarization. When these features are analyzed for any indication of arrhythmia, the size and shape of each curve is examined (see side box). Any damage to the pacemaker cells of the SA node may require implantation of an electrical pacemaker to maintain the proper rhythm of heartbeats.

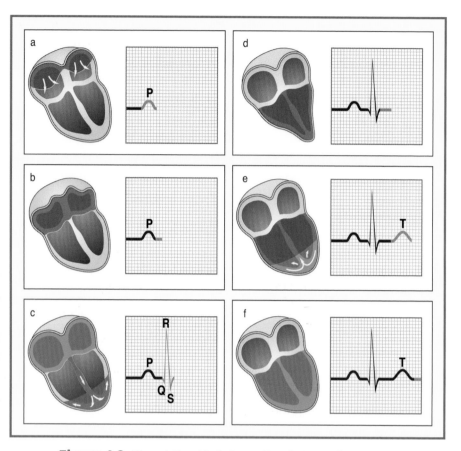

Figure 6.3 The relationship between the electrocardiogram and the electrical activity of the heart is illustrated here. The portions of the heart that are in depolarization and are therefore being stimulated to contract are shown in red. Green represents the initiation of repolarization (relaxation phase).

THE CARDIAC CYCLE

One complete cardiac cycle represents all of the events that occur in sequence from the start of one heartbeat until the start of the next. Examining this complete cycle will allow us to better understand and coordinate the electrical activity of the heart with its corresponding contractile functions. Fluids, like blood, will only move from one region to another if a pressure gradient exists. For blood to move from an atrium to a ventricle, therefore, blood pressure in the atrium must be higher than the pressure in the ventricle. The flow of blood between these two chambers will stop once the pressures are equal. The heart valves prevent blood from flowing from the ventricles back into atria.

IRREGULAR HEART RHYTHMS

Because the ECG records the electrical activity of the heart, it can also be used to detect irregularities in heart rhythm. The ECG can determine, for example, whether the heart is beating too fast, a condition called **tachycardia**, or too slow, a condition known as **bradycardia**, by measuring the amount of time elapsed from one QRS complex to the next.

A cardiac patient may exhibit particularly dangerous forms of tachycardia in the ventricles of the heart known as ventricular flutter or fibrillation. These forms of tachycardia typically occur when an area of the ventricle becomes autorhythmic, overriding the slower signal arriving from the SA node. Ventricular tachycardia can cause the ventricles to contract as many as 300 times per minute, a rate too fast to effectively move blood through the circulatory system. Rapid intervention is required with this condition to prevent complete heart failure.

Other types of irregularities may involve a block in the conducting pathway that relays the electrical signal from the SA node to the ventricular muscle, potentially resulting in a loss of coordination between atrial and ventricular contractions. A prolonged P-R interval, the amount of time elapsed between the P and R waves, may indicate blockage in the AV node.

Ischemia, a decrease in the blood supply in the heart, may show up on an ECG as an inverted T wave, where the T wave is reflected downward rather than upward. In addition, if a heart attack occurs, in which blood flow and oxygen supply to a region of the heart are reduced significantly for a period of time, an ECG can help a cardiologist identify which area of the heart muscle was affected as well as the extent of the damage.

The cardiac cycle can be divided into phases of contraction, known as **systole** (pronounced sis-toe-lee), and relaxation, or **diastole** (pronounced die-as-toe-lee), for each of the chambers. Periods of systole are important for generating the blood pressures necessary for moving blood. Diastole is important to ensure that there is enough relaxation time to refill the chambers with blood before the next contraction. The timing of atrial systole and ventricular systole is important. Atrial systole must precede ventricular systole to ensure adequate time to fill the ventricles fully before they begin contraction.

Figure 6.4 illustrates the events of the cardiac cycle. Using this diagram, the key features of an ECG can be correlated with the changes in pressure within the heart chambers and with changes in the blood volume within each of these chambers.

The P wave correlates with the start of atrial contraction or systole. When ventricular systole begins and atrial systole ends, the QRS complex appears. The ventricles end systole and start diastole, indicated by the T wave. There is a relatively long period when both the atria and ventricles are in diastole, and there is no detectable electrical activity.

If the electrical events and phases are matched with pressure changes within the heart chambers, a picture of what occurs during atrial and ventricular systole begins to emerge.

The left side of the heart must eject blood out of the heart against the high pressure that exists within the systemic circuit. This pressure, represented on the graph by the aortic pressure, varies between 90 and 120 mm Hg during the course of one cardiac cycle. After the QRS complex appears and ventricular systole starts, pressure begins to build within the ventricle as its muscular walls squeeze down on the volume of blood within. As soon as the pressure within the ventricle exceeds the pressure in the aorta, the aortic semilunar valves open and blood is forcibly ejected into the aorta (causing its pressure to rise).

As the volume of blood decreases within the left ventricle, its pressure starts to decrease. Once ventricular pressure is below aortic pressure, the semilunar valve closes, and no more blood is moved. The ventricle then relaxes, allowing the relaxed heart to refill with blood.

The pressure changes in the right atrium and ventricle are perfectly coordinated with the events in the left atrium and ventricle. The right and left sides of the heart contract and relax in concert. The difference between the right and left heart is the pressure against which they must eject their respective volumes of blood. Aortic pressure varies between 90 and 120 mm Hg, but pulmonary artery pressures are much lower, typically from 10 to 25 mm Hg. When right ventricular pressure exceeds that of the pulmonary aorta, the pulmonary semilunar valves open and blood is ejected into the pulmonary circuit.

HEART SOUNDS

During each cardiac cycle, two heart major sounds can be heard using a stethoscope. These sounds are associated with the closing of the heart valves. (A third sound is occasionally heard in children but is rarely audible in adults.) The first heart sound occurs when the AV valves between the atria and ventricles close at the start of ventricular systole (see Figure 6.4, bottom). This sound tends to be louder than the second sound. The second major heart sound occurs at the end of ventricular systole when the semilunar valves close.

MEASURES OF HEART FUNCTION

Cardiac output, or **CO**, is the volume of blood ejected by each ventricle in one minute. It indicates the level of efficiency of the heart as a pump. Cardiac output is the product of the **heart rate (HR)** times the **stroke volume (SV)**. The stroke volume is the volume of blood pumped out by a ventricle with each beat. For example, if the heart rate is 65 beats per minute (or bpm) and the stroke volume is 75 milliliters per beat, then cardiac output will equal 4,875 milliliters per minute (ml/min), or about 4.9 liters per minute (L/min).

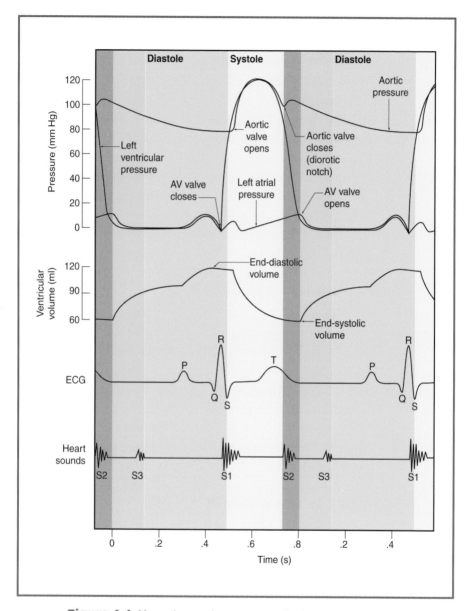

Figure 6.4 Many changes in pressure and volume accompany the cardiac cycle. The major changes can be seen in this diagram. The events are shown in coordination with a typical electrocardiogram (ECG) recording and the major heart sounds as detected by a stethoscope. Two complete cardiac cycles are depicted in this figure.

The stroke volume can be calculated by subtracting the volume at the end of ventricular systole (the end-systolic volume, or ESV) from the volume present at the start of the contraction phase (the end-diastolic volume, or EDV). Note that the volume of blood in the ventricle starts to increase as the ventricle refills with blood with the onset of ventricular diastole.

In a resting individual, at the start of a new cardiac cycle, there is about 60 ml of blood remaining from the previous cycle; this is the end-systolic volume. Another 30 ml is added passively as blood returns to the atria and flows through the open AV valves into the ventricles. Atrial systole adds another 40 ml to the volume in the ventricles, for a total of 130 ml, the end-diastolic volume. Once the stroke volume of 70 ml is ejected during ventricular systole, there is 60 ml left, the end-systolic volume, which is the starting point.

Adjustments to both stroke volume and heart rate are made to maintain an adequate supply of blood to the tissues. With heavy exercise, for example, cardiac output can increase from roughly 5 L/min to 18–40 L/min, depending on an individual's level of fitness. This increase is achieved primarily through an increase in the heart rate and also in the stroke volume.

Any changes in the EDV and/or the ESV of the ventricle will affect the stroke volume. (Recall that the stroke volume = EDV–ESV.) The EDV is affected by the time available for filling of the ventricle. As the heart rate speeds up, there is less time between contractions for blood to fill the ventricles. The EDV is also dependent on the rate of return of blood to the heart by the venous system, known as **venous return**. If the EDV remains unchanged, then any decrease in EDV will cause the SV to decrease, while an increase in EDV will result in an increased SV.

At rest, the stroke volume is less than 55% of the EDV, a percentage called the ejection fraction. The remaining blood, about 60 ml, is the ESV. With strenuous exercise in trained athletes, the ejection fraction can be increased to as much as 90% of the EDV, significantly reducing the ESV. The ejection fraction is an important measure of cardiac function.

It should be noted that the stroke volumes for the right and left ventricles are the same (i.e., they both eject the same volume of blood with every contraction of the heart). A mismatch between the stroke volumes can lead to severe health problems and is a condition known as **congestive heart failure.** If, for example, left heart function is reduced and leads to a reduction in stroke volume, blood backs up in the lungs, forcing fluid into the interstitium and making it very difficult to breathe. Similarly, right heart failure leads to systemic edema, the accumulation of fluid in the systemic interstitium, as blood backs up in the systemic circuit.

CONNECTIONS

The heart generates its own rhythm for contraction. Pacemaker cells in the sinoatrial (SA) node relay a signal through the conducting system of the heart. Other structures in this conducting system help to coordinate the contractions that this signal elicits. For example, the AV node delays transmission of the signal to the ventricles, allowing time for atrial contraction and ventricular filling.

The cardiac cycle represents the changes in pressure and volume that accompany atrial and ventricular diastole and systole. While the volume of blood ejected by the right and left ventricles (the stroke volume) is identical, the pressures generated by each ventricle differ greatly. The left ventricle must pump its stroke volume against the much higher pressure of the systemic circuit. Pumping blood against the lower pressure within the pulmonary circuit requires less work by the right ventricle.

Cardiac output is an important measure of heart function and is determined by multiplying the heart rate times the stroke volume. Hence, changes in cardiac output can be achieved through alterations in either of these two variables. Chapter 8 provides two examples of how cardiac output is affected by challenges to circulation, in the forms of hemorrhage and exercise.

7

The Control of Blood Pressure and Distribution

Blood pressure is important to the proper functioning of the circulatory system. Blood will not move unless it is under pressure. The heart generates the pressure that drives the blood through the entire system of blood vessels, reaching every part of the body. When a doctor or nurse checks your blood pressure, he or she is gaining valuable information about how your circulatory system is working. The two numbers that are recorded after the cuff is wrapped around your arm and inflated indicate whether your blood pressure is normal, too high, or too low. But what exactly do these numbers mean, and what is "too high" or "too low"?

BLOOD PRESSURE

Blood flow, and therefore blood pressure, within all arteries occurs in waves, or pulses, in synchronization with the cardiac cycle. Blood pressure is highest during ventricular systole, when blood is being forced into the arteries. Arterial blood pressures are lowest during ventricular diastole, when the heart is refilling with blood. These two pressures represent the two numbers when blood pressure is recorded. The higher number, typically less than 120 mm Hg in a healthy person, is the systolic blood pressure. The lower number, usually less than 80 mm Hg, is the diastolic pressure. These numbers are stated as systolic over diastolic pressure (e.g., 110 over 70 mm Hg would be an example of a "healthy" blood pressure reading).

Measuring the blood pressure using a **blood pressure cuff** makes use of the principles of Boyle's law. The cuff is inflated to a pressure well above that of the higher systolic pressure, blocking flow within the vessel. As the pressure is slowly released, a sound will be heard as blood begins to squirt through during ventricular systole. At this point, the pressure in the cuff equals the systolic pressure. As cuff pressure is reduced further, the sounds will disappear once the brachial artery (the major artery running down the arm) is fully open and blood flow is no longer interrupted at any point in the cardiac cycle. The pressure at which the sounds disappear represents your diastolic pressure.

FACTORS AFFECTING BLOOD PRESSURE

As you learned in the previous chapter, the heart generates the pressure that moves blood through its circuits. One of the factors that affects blood pressure is heart function, or cardiac output. Cardiac output is a measure of the efficiency of the heart and indicates how much blood volume the heart is pumping per unit of time, typically in ml/min. If either stroke volume or heart rate increases (see Chapter 6), then cardiac output increases. When cardiac output increases, blood pressure also rises. Conversely, if either stroke volume or heart rate decreases, blood pressure will decrease as well.

Other factors that affect blood pressure include blood volume, total peripheral resistance, and blood viscosity. As the volume of blood within the circulatory system increases, blood pressure increases. If an individual begins

THE BAROMETER FOR BLOOD PRESSURE DROPS

In 2003, the definition of "healthy" blood pressure changed. For years, a systolic pressure of 120 mm Hg with a diastolic pressure of 80 mm Hg was considered to be "healthy." The National Heart, Lung, and Blood Institute has now categorized systolic pressures of 120 to 149 mm Hg and diastolic pressures of 80 to 90 mm Hg as "prehypertension," meaning an individual with these values is at risk for developing hypertension, or high blood pressure. This change means that 45 million previously "healthy" individuals must now make some lifestyle changes, such as losing weight and exercising, to reduce their blood pressure. Table 7.1 lists the revised guidelines for blood pressure recordings and includes recommended treatments for two stages of hypertension. The new classifications are a result of recent scientific studies demonstrating that an increased risk of heart disease occurs with blood pressures lower than previously believed.

One-third of Americans with hypertension are undiagnosed and completely unaware they have this dangerous condition. Hypertension places an individual at increased risk for heart attacks, strokes, kidney failure, and heart failure, all potentially lethal conditions. For this reason, hypertension is called the silent killer, because individuals may not know they have the disease until after they suffer serious damage.

Those classified with prehypertension are more likely to develop hypertension and heart disease and need to take action. For every 20-point rise in systolic pressure above 115 mm Hg or 10-point rise in diastolic pressure above 75 mm Hg, the risk for heart disease doubles. Medication is not recommended for prehypertension. Instead, officials recommend that these individuals lose weight if they are overweight, avoid excess salt, stay physically active, stop smoking, and limit their alcohol consumption. Because blood pressure values typically rise with age as arteries become more rigid and lose their elasticity, older Americans need to be more vigilant in following these recommendations.

About 50 million Americans have been diagnosed with hypertension, but officials estimate that 2/3 of these patients do not have their high blood pressure under control. The new guidelines also make recommendations for treatment. These recommendations differ based on the severity of the hypertension, Stage I or II, and whether other conditions exist or not. Health officials found that one of the most effective medications for hypertension, a class of drugs known as diuretics, is also one of the cheapest to prescribe.

Diuretics, like the drug furosemide (or Lasix®), act on the kidney to increase urine volume, thereby reducing blood volume and blood pressure. Low-salt diets are likewise recommended for reducing and preventing hypertension. The ingestion of salt promotes thirst and drinking, expanding blood volume and raising blood pressure until the kidney has time to correct the volume overload.

Pressure in mm Hg	Normal	Prehypertension	Stage I Hypertension	Stage II Hypertension
Systolic	Less than 120	120–139	140–159	More than 160
Diastolic	Less than 80	80–89	90–99	More than 100
Drug Treatment				
Only Condition	None	None	Diuretics, occasionally other drugs	Two-drug combo; typically one is a diurectic
Other Conditions*	None	Treat Other Diseases	Multiple Medications	Multiple Medications

* Treatments for hypertension with other conditions are only approved for patients 18 and older.

Table 7.1 New guidelines for blood pressure as recommended by the National Heart, Lung, and Blood Institute, 2003.

to lose blood, due to a major injury, for example, his or her blood pressure will also drop. In such a case, the immediate replacement of the lost blood with a blood transfusion can help to restore blood pressure. Loss of blood pressure can mean insufficient blood flow to the body's tissues and the subsequent lack of oxygen can cause permanent damage or death.

Total peripheral resistance, or TPR, is a measure of the degree of resistance to blood flow within the blood vessels and is related to the vessel diameter. Arterioles are considered to be the resistance vessels of the circulatory system. When these vessels vasoconstrict, their diameters decrease, generating a greater degree of friction between the flowing blood and the vessel walls, and increasing the TPR. Conversely, when these vessels vasodilate, their diameters increase, reducing the amount of friction between blood and the vessel walls, and decreasing the TPR. Blood pressure must exceed this force of friction, or resistance to flow, for the flow to continue. For this reason, with an increase in peripheral resistance, the blood pressure increases. Blood pressure drops in response to vasodilation and reduced peripheral resistance.

Blood is primarily water, but it also contains cells and proteins (see Chapter 3). The viscosity of blood is a measure of its "thickness." The higher the viscosity of the blood, the greater its resistance to flow, and more energy or pressure is required to propel it through the circulatory system. Usually the viscosity of blood remains constant, but there are conditions that can cause it to increase, leading to an increase in blood pressure. Likewise, a decrease in viscosity will lead to a decrease in blood pressure.

The important relationship between cardiac output, total peripheral resistance, and blood pressure (actually mean arterial blood pressure) can be expressed in the formula:

Blood Pressure = Cardiac Output x Total Peripheral Resistance

Using this formula, one can predict how a change in cardiac output or peripheral resistance will affect blood pressure.

BLOOD PRESSURES THROUGHOUT THE CIRCULATORY SYSTEM

The measurement of blood pressure indicates the *arterial* blood pressure. Blood pressure must reside within all of our blood vessels, however, because this is the force that moves blood continuously through the circulatory system. As a fluid, blood will only move in the presence of a pressure gradient and always flows from a region of higher pressure to a region of lower pressure. Blood pressure decreases as the distance from the left ventricle increases. Pressures are highest in the arteries, and decrease as blood moves to the venous side of the system. This pressure difference exists so that blood moves in only one direction, from the arterial to the venous side and back to the heart.

As you learned in Chapter 5, arteries and veins have, on average, much larger diameters than capillaries. However, the total cross-sectional area (the number of vessels and their diameters) of the capillaries is much greater than that of either the arteries or veins.

The rate of blood flow is fast through the larger arteries, where pressure is high and resistance to flow is low. In contrast, after branching numerous times, the rate of blood flow as it approaches the capillaries has slowed significantly. Recall that the capillaries are the site of exchange of materials between the blood and the tissues. The slower rate of blood flow allows adequate time for **capillary exchange** to occur.

CAPILLARY EXCHANGE

To accommodate capillary exchange, the walls of the capillaries are extremely thin, consisting of a single-layer of endothelial cells with a basement membrane. In the capillaries, materials are exchanged through the process of diffusion. Water, ions, glucose, amino acids, and the waste product urea pass through the endothelial cell junctions according to their concentration gradients. Larger molecules, blood proteins, and cells are too large to move through the cell junctions and are, therefore, retained within the capillaries.

Diffusion is not the only process involved in the movement of materials across the capillary wall. The pressure differences between the blood and the interstitial compartment (the fluid surrounding the tissue cells) promote the movement of fluid between the endothelial cell junctions into the tissues, a process known as **filtration**. Because blood pressure decreases along the length of the capillary, the rate of filtration decreases as well. Filtration is highest at the arterial end of the capillary and lowest at the venous end.

Another process, called **reabsorption**, counteracts filtration. Reabsorption describes the movement of fluid from the interstitium back into the capillary. As water and dissolved solutes move via diffusion and filtration from the blood into the interstitium, the remaining solutes and particularly the proteins increase in concentration.

Water moves, via a specialized form of diffusion known as osmosis, across membranes down an osmotic gradient or from a region of low solute concentration to one of higher solute concentration.

To summarize, filtration forces water and solutes out of the capillary and into the interstitium, while reabsorption promotes the movement of water and solutes from the interstitium back into the capillary. The balance of these two opposing forces changes along the length of the capillary. In the initial portion of the capillary, the rate of filtration exceeds the rate of reabsorption. However, toward the venous end of the capillary, as more and more fluid leaves

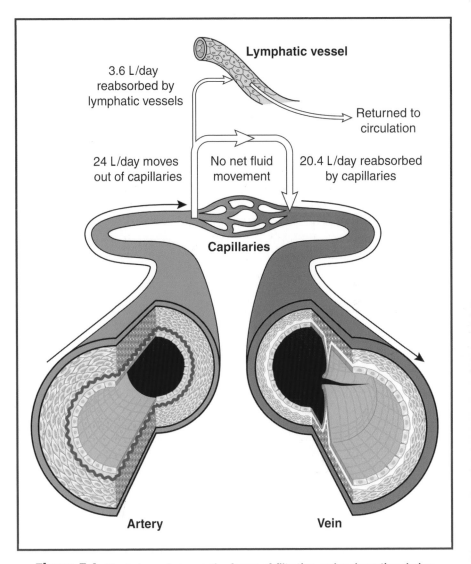

Figure 7.1 The balance between the forces of filtration and reabsorption during capillary exchange is illustrated here. Filtration, or the movement of fluid into the interstitium, occurs when blood pressure within the capillary is greater than interstitial pressure. The rate of filtration diminishes as you progress toward the venous end of the capillary. Reabsorption, or the movement of fluid from the interstitium back into the capillary, is due to the increased solute concentrations of the blood. Reabsorption is favored over filtration toward the venous end of the capillary. Any excess fluid remaining in the interstitium is returned to circulation through the lymphatic system.

the capillary, the rate of reabsorption is greater than the rate of filtration. Typically, the lymphatic system picks up any excess fluid remaining in the interstitium, returning it to circulation near the heart (Figure 7.1).

Any condition that affects the blood pressure, the interstitial pressure, or the osmotic pressure of the blood can alter the dynamic balance between the forces of filtration and reabsorption. For example, with **kwashiorkor**, a protein deficiency disease, the osmotic pressure of the blood is low because of a lack of blood proteins. As a result, the rate of reabsorption by the capillaries is greatly reduced and unable to effectively counteract filtration. Fluid accumulates in the interstitium, leading to a condition known as edema and the appearance of a swollen belly.

If blood pressure decreases, perhaps in response to blood loss as with **hemorrhage**, capillary filtration will be reduced. In this case, reabsorption will dominate and fluid that is residing in the interstitium will move into circulation. In this way, interstitial fluid serves as a reserve of fluid for replacing blood when blood volume drops.

VENOUS RETURN

Venous pressure is an important determinant of venous return (the amount of blood returned to the heart) and cardiac output. The rate of flow in the veins increases as blood flows from the smaller diameter venules and veins to larger veins with greater diameters and lower resistance to flow.

In a standing person, gravity must be overcome to return blood from the region of the body below the heart. How can venous return be accomplished in an upright person, given the low pressure gradients found in the venous system and the pull of gravity? As described previously, contractions of the skeletal muscles, also known as the **skeletal muscle pump**, can compress the veins and help squeeze the blood past one-way valves that prevent backflow. In addition, venous return is aided by what is called the **respiratory pump**.

When a person expands the chest cavity to take a breath, the pressure within that cavity is decreased. This action lowers the pressures in the largest vessels returning blood to the heart, creating a more favorable pressure gradient for blood to flow toward the heart. In addition, neural input can help with venous return by stimulating vasoconstriction in these capacitance vessels.

REGULATION OF CIRCULATORY FUNCTION

One of the primary functions of the circulatory system is to deliver oxygen-rich blood to the body's tissues. The oxygen is used by cells to make ATP (energy) in a process called cellular respiration. A waste product of cellular respiration is carbon dioxide, which must be removed efficiently or it may adversely affect acid-base balance. The circulatory system must also remove harmful nitrogenous waste products like urea.

Changes in cardiac output, peripheral resistance, and blood pressure play a role in how the circulatory system adjusts to ensure that the oxygen demands of the tissues are matched by an adequate supply of oxygen-rich blood. To ensure that the responses of the circulatory system are made in a coordinated and appropriate manner, there are multiple levels of control and feedback.

Some control occurs on a local level. For example, if a particular tissue is not obtaining an adequate supply of blood, it can signal to increase the blood flow to just that particular region. This form of control is called **autoregulation**, and the increase in local flow is achieved through the release of vasodilators. Vasodilators, such as carbon dioxide and lactic acid, act locally to dilate the precapillary sphincters in nearby capillary beds, thus enhancing blood flow only to the specific region affected.

Vasoconstrictors may also be released locally. Their presence causes the precapillary sphincters to vasoconstrict, cutting off the blood flow to the affected capillary beds. Vasoconstricting substances are most often released when the vessel wall is damaged. Activated platelets adhering to the damaged tissue release these vasoconstrictors, thereby reducing blood loss at the site of injury.

In addition to local control, there is also neural control of circulatory function. It is important, for example, that while blood flow is diverted to one tissue to meet its increased oxygen demand, another important tissue is not being deprived of its blood flow. Both cardiac output and total peripheral resistance are regulated by the nervous system. Located within the medulla oblongata of the brain stem are the cardiovascular centers, groups of neurons that regulate these two important variables. They discharge two different types of neural information: sympathetic and parasympathetic output. In general, these two forms of neural output have opposing effects on the target tissue.

Another method of regulation is through **baroreceptors**, stretch receptors located in the walls of the carotid arteries and the aortic arch that sense changes in blood pressure (Figure 7.2). A decrease in the firing rate of the baroreceptors signals a drop in blood pressure to the medullary cardiovascular center in the brain. This center also receives input from **chemoreceptors** in the aortic arch and carotid arteries. The chemoreceptors alert the center if carbon dioxide levels in the blood become elevated. In either case, the response to elevated blood carbon dioxide levels or a drop in blood pressure is the same, since both variables signal that perfusion of the tissues is compromised. Increased sympathetic output to the sinoatrial node of the heart causes the heart rate to increase. Stroke volume is enhanced because

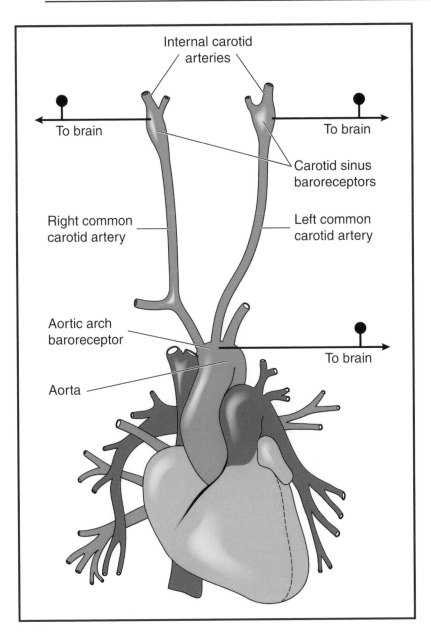

Figure 7.2 Baroreceptors located in the carotid arteries and aortic arch change their rate of firing in response to changes in blood pressure. This information is relayed to the cardiovascular center located in the medulla oblongata of the brain stem.

of an increase in contractility of the heart muscle, again in response to a sympathetic discharge from the center. Sympathetic discharge from the center to the veins results in vasoconstriction and enhanced venous return to support the increase in cardiac output. Vasoconstriction in the systemic arterioles is also mediated by sympathetic outflow from the center, raising the total peripheral resistance.

Changes in circulatory function can also be initiated by certain hormones, in addition to local and neural control. The heart and blood vessels can respond directly to circulating hormones through the presence of hormone receptors in these tissues. Thyroid hormone, for example, increases the heart rate. Likewise, other circulating chemicals in the blood can alter circulatory function. Stimulants, such as caffeine and nicotine, elevate the heart rate by enhancing the impact of the neurotransmitters released by the sympathetic system.

CONNECTIONS

Blood pressure represents the critical force that powers the circulation of blood through the tissues. Blood pressure is affected by a variety of factors including cardiac output (through changes in stroke volume and/or heart rate), blood volume, blood viscosity, and total peripheral resistance.

Blood pressure and the rate of blood flow vary throughout the circulatory system. Blood pressures and flow rates are high in the arteries. Flow rates are particularly low in the capillaries. There is a great increase in the resistance to flow in these vessels because of their large number and small diameter. The slower flow allows adequate time for the process of capillary exchange.

There are a variety of controls on circulatory function. Local control ensures that individual tissues can meet their oxygen needs by adjusting their blood supply. However, the nervous system plays the key regulatory role in circulatory function through the coordination of blood flow to the various tissues. Baroreceptors provide information about blood pressure to the cardiovascular center in the medulla, which acts to make the appropriate adjustments through changes in sympathetic and parasympathetic output to the heart and blood vessels.

8

Circulatory Responses to Hemorrhage and Exercise

Knowing how the circulatory system functions normally is important in learning how the system operates under other conditions, such as after an injury or during exercise. One of the best ways to underscore how the circulatory system functions is to challenge that system to adapt to a new physiological situation. To understand this concept, we will first examine how the human body attempts to counteract the deleterious effects of severe hemorrhage, or major blood loss.

CIRCULATORY RESPONSES TO HEMORRHAGE

A hemorrhage is a significant loss of blood volume, either externally or internally. Internal bleeding is often difficult to detect, but still requires immediate attention. Once a significant volume of blood is lost from circulation, the effects can be truly life-threatening.

The loss of blood causes a decrease in venous return to the heart and subsequently a decrease in stroke volume, the amount of blood pumped by the heart with each contraction. As a result, cardiac output is reduced. A decrease in cardiac output will cause a decrease in blood pressure (Figure 8.1).

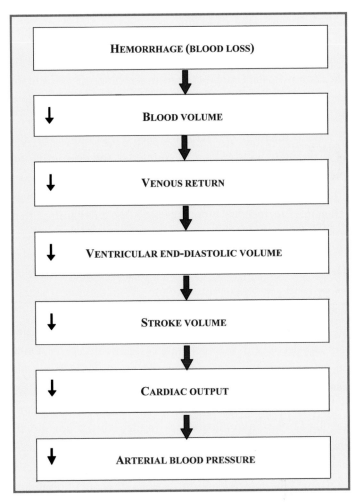

Figure 8.1 Factors leading to a drop in blood pressure with hemorrhage are illustrated here. The loss of blood volume leads to a decrease in venous pressure and return to the heart is reduced. A reduction in venous return causes a decrease in cardiac output and arterial blood pressure.

Blood pressure, the force that moves blood throughout the circulatory system, must be restored to a level that allows for adequate perfusion of the tissues so they do not become oxygen-starved and suffer irreversible damage. The drop in blood pressure will be sensed by the baroreceptors, which decrease their rate of firing as blood pressure drops.

Changes in the firing rate of the baroreceptors are sensed by the cardiovascular center of the medulla oblongata of the brain stem. A suite of homeostatic mechanisms will be set into motion to help return blood pressure level to normal.

Using the formula described earlier, it is possible to predict how the body will respond to counteract the drop in blood pressure that accompanies hemorrhage. Recall that Blood Pressure = Cardiac Output x Total Peripheral Resistance. Therefore, to increase blood pressure, the mechanisms that promote an increase in cardiac output and/or total peripheral resistance would be called into action. Because Cardiac Output = Heart Rate x Stroke Volume, it becomes evident that increasing either heart rate and/or stroke volume should also help restore adequate blood pressure.

As discussed in Chapter 7, the drop in blood pressure causes a decrease in the firing rate of the baroreceptors. Once this decreased firing rate is sensed by the cardiovascular center, it reduces its parasympathetic output and increases its sympathetic output, resulting in an increase in sympathetic stimulation to the SA node in the right atrium and an increase in heart rate (Figure 8.2). Stroke volume increases and sympathetic stimulation of the cardiac muscle elicits more forceful ventricular contractions. A greater volume of blood is ejected with each heartbeat. An increase in cardiac output was initiated through increased stroke volume and heart rate.

The medullary cardiovascular center also increases its sympathetic input to certain blood vessels. Veins are called capacitance vessels, because at any one time a large percentage of the circulating blood volume is within these vessels. Increased sympathetic stimulation of the veins results in vasoconstriction, forcing some of the blood volume within these vessels into the rest of the circulatory system. This action increases venous return to the heart, elevating stroke volume via a different mechanism. Keeping a hemorrhaging individual

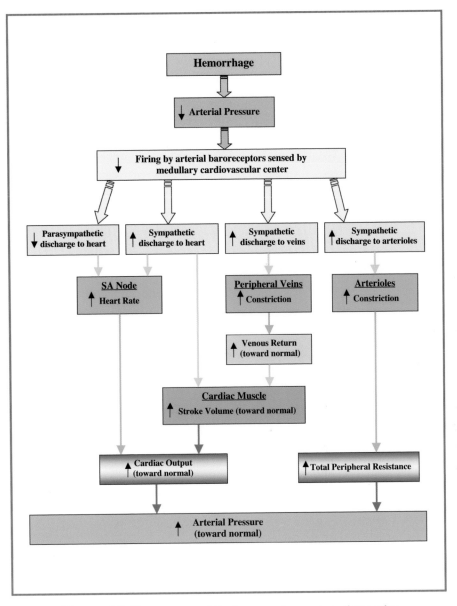

Figure 8.2 The response of the baroreceptors and cardiovascular centers to a decrease in blood pressure is illustrated in this flow chart. Increased sympathetic discharge to the heart, veins, and arterioles triggers changes that help return blood pressure toward the normal range.

lying down also aids venous return to the heart, as it reduces gravitational pull on the blood returning from the lower body regions.

Finally, sympathetic output from the cardiovascular center also acts directly on the arterioles, which are also called resistance vessels. Recall that small changes in the diameter of these vessels can have a huge impact on blood pressure. In this case, increased sympathetic discharge induces vasoconstriction of the arterioles, causing total peripheral resistance to rise.

To summarize, a drop in blood pressure results in increased sympathetic discharge from the medullary cardiovascular center to the SA node, the cardiac muscle, the veins, and arterioles. The net result is an increased cardiac output and total peripheral resistance, leading to an increase in blood pressure.

Hormonal responses also play a role. Increased levels of angiotensin II and antidiuretic hormone promote vasoconstriction and elevate total peripheral resistance. Both hormones also promote restoration of blood volume as they induce a powerful sense of thirst.

CIRCULATORY RESPONSES TO EXERCISE

To meet the increased oxygen needs of active tissues, cardiac output must increase. The output can increase from a resting rate of 5 liters per minute to a value as high as 35 liters per minute in athletes. The increase in cardiac output is accomplished primarily through an increase in heart rate. Stroke volume also increases, though to a lesser degree, with exercise.

The distribution of blood flow changes as a person goes from the resting to the active state. Increased flow to the exercising muscles, the skin, and the heart is achieved through vasodilation of the vessels in those organs (Figure 8.3). The exercising muscles and heart require more oxygen for their increased activity levels, and the flow to the skin helps to unload excess body heat. At the same time, flow to the digestive system

	Rest (ml/min)	Strenuous Exercise (ml/min)
Brain	650 (13%)	750 (4%)
Heart	215 (4%)	750 (4%)
Skeletal Muscle	1,030 (20%)	12,500 (73%)
Skin	430 (9%)	1,900 (11%)
Kidney	950 (20%)	600 (3%)
Abdominal Organs	1,200 (24%)	600 (3%)
Other	525 (10%)	400 (2%)
Total	5,000	17,500

Figure 8.3 The distribution of blood flow changes as an individual goes from a resting to a strenuously active state. There is increased flow to the heart, active skeletal muscles, and skin (to facilitate heat loss), while blood flow to the abdominal organs and kidneys is decreased. (Percentages represent total blood flow.)

and kidneys is reduced because the nervous system stimulates vasoconstriction in these tissues.

Overall, blood pressure increases by a small amount with exercise. Although cardiac output increases, total peripheral resistance drops due to widespread vasodilation. In this way, the drop in total peripheral resistance mostly offsets the rise in cardiac output; hence, blood pressure increases only a small degree.

Venous return, or the return of blood to the heart, must also

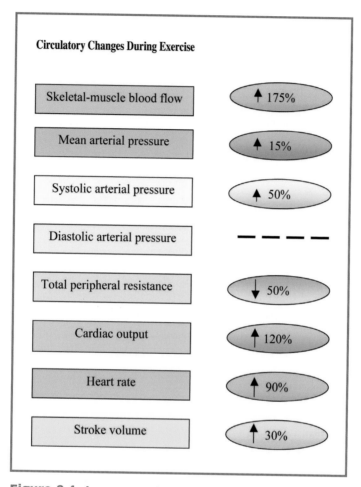

Figure 8.4 A summary of some of the short-term circulatory changes that occur with exercise is shown here. Total peripheral resistance decreases with exercise due to vasodilation. Blood pressure, heart rate, cardiac output, and stroke volume all increase, helping to increase blood flow to the active skeletal muscles.

increase to maintain a high cardiac output. Increased venous return with exercise is aided by several mechanisms, including increased sympathetic output to the veins, stimulating vaso-constriction in those vessels. As with hemorrhage, this response helps to reduce the volume of blood carried by the veins, forcing that volume toward the heart. In addition, the skeletal muscle and respiratory pumps are more active with exercise, increasing venous return and cardiac output.

The nervous system plays a key role in the circulatory responses to exercise. In fact, the mere anticipation of exercise can induce certain circulatory responses before an individual even begins to exercise. For example, increased sympathetic and decreased parasympathetic input to the heart from the medullary cardiovascular center enhances cardiac output prior to exercise. With exercise, increased sympathetic output to the arterioles lowers total peripheral resistance and increased sympathetic output to the veins increases venous return with exercise.

Local mechanisms play a role as well. As activity increases, the partial pressure of oxygen of the exercising tissue decreases and the partial pressure of carbon dioxide and acidity levels increases. These changes signal a need for increased blood flow to these regions. Vasodilation of the blood vessels in these tissues allows for increased flow to meet the change in oxygen demand. In addition, the Bohr effect will enhance the unloading of oxygen from hemoglobin circulating through these tissues. Figure 8.4 summarizes many of the short-term changes in circulatory function that accompany exercise.

With years of physical exercise, long-term changes in circulatory function can occur. Training increases an individual's maximum cardiac output, the factor which most often limits the ability of the body to meet the increased oxygen demands required to meet an increase in workload. Long-term physical training has a significant impact on stroke volume. An increased stroke volume is achieved through enhanced pumping ability of the heart. The ventricular walls thicken, contract more forcibly, and eject more blood with each heart beat. As a consequence, the degree to which the heart rate is elevated for a given workload is reduced in trained athletes (Figure 8.5). Venous return is enhanced as well through an overall increase in blood volume.

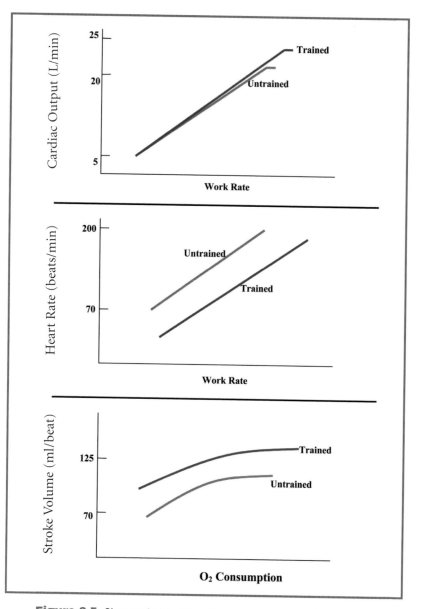

Figure 8.5 Changes in heart function accompany extensive physical training. With training, there is an increase in the maximum cardiac output that can be achieved. The heart will not strain as hard to pump blood to the body, so heart rate is decreased with training. Stroke volume is enhanced with training, reducing the demand on heart rate.

In addition, an increase in the number of mitochondria as well as the enzymes of cellular respiration occurs within the skeletal muscles involved in training. As a consequence, these muscles use oxygen and fuel more efficiently, improving their endurance.

CONNECTIONS

Examining how the human circulatory system adjusts to challenges helps us to better understand how the system works. With hemorrhage, the loss of blood volume leads to a decrease in blood pressure that must be returned to normal to prevent tissue damage and death. Massive sympathetic output by the cardiovascular center of the medulla triggers homeostatic mechanisms that contribute to reversing the decrease in blood pressure. Direct effects on the SA node and cardiac muscle enhance cardiac output. Vasoconstriction of the veins increases venous return, while vasoconstriction of the systemic arterioles raises the total peripheral resistance.

Short-term circulatory responses to exercise are primarily achieved through the actions of the cardiovascular center as well, although local control plays a role in ensuring that the more active tissues receive an adequate blood supply. The increase in cardiac output seen with exercise is primarily accomplished through an increase in heart rate. With long-term physical training, however, stroke volume will also be enhanced.

The distribution of blood flow to organs is altered with exercise. Flow to the active tissues, the heart, and skin is increased, while flow to the kidneys and digestive system is reduced. Venous return is enhanced through the increased activity of the skeletal muscle and respiratory pumps and vasoconstriction in the veins. Blood pressure is only slightly elevated with exercise, as the increase in cardiac output is off-set by a drop in total peripheral resistance due to widespread vasodilation.

Glossary

Affinity Ability of a molecule to bind a substrate.

Albumins A class of blood plasma proteins.

Anemia Low red-blood-cell count.

Angina Any disease characterized by spasmodic suffocative attacks—
for example, angina pectoris, paroxysmal thoracic pain with feeling
of suffocation.

Angioplasty Also called percutaneous transluminal coronary angioplasty
(PTCA). Dilation of a plaque-lined artery to increase blood flow by
insertion of catheter with deflated balloon at its tip into narrowed
artery. Once inserted, the balloon is inflated, compressing the plaque
and enlarging the inner diameter of the blood vessel.

Antibody Substance produced by the body that destroys or inactivates
a specific substance (antigen) that has entered the body.

Antigen Substance that, when introduced into the body, causes formation
of antibodies against it.

Aortic Semilunar Valve Heart valve that separates the left ventricle
from the ascending aorta.

Arrhythmia Abnormal heartbeat.

Arteries Muscular blood vessels that carry blood away from the heart.

Arterioles Small muscular blood vessels that deliver blood to the
capillaries.

Ascending Aorta The initial portion of the aortic arch into which
blood is forced by the left ventricle.

Atherosclerosis A condition in which fatty plaques form on the walls
of arteries, also known as hardening of the arteries.

Atria Plural of atrium. *See* **atrium.**

Atrioventricular (AV) Node Small mass of special cardiac muscle tissue located in the right atrium along the lower part of the interatrial
septum.

Atrioventricular Valves Also known as AV valves, flaps of tissue that
separate the atria from the ventricles.

Atrium Chamber of the heart that receives blood returning to the heart.

Autoregulation Self regulation.

Autorhythmic Capable of spontaneously depolarizing and generating a rhythm.

Baroreceptors Arterial sensory receptors that sense changes in blood pressure.

Basophils A type of granulocyte (white blood cell) that releases histamine and contributes to inflammation.

Bicuspid Valve An alternative name for the left atrioventricular valve.

Blood The fluid connective tissue that circulates within the blood vessels and heart.

Blood Pressure Cuff Apparatus (also called a sphygmomanometer) used to measure blood pressure by measuring the amount of air pressure equal to the blood pressure in an artery.

Bohr Effect The reduction in hemoglobin's affinity for oxygen due to decreasing pH or increasing CO_2 levels.

Bradycardia Abnormally slow heart rate.

Bulk Flow Movement of fluids like air and water from a region of high pressure to a region of low pressure.

Capacitance Vessels Blood vessels, like the veins, that hold a significant portion of the blood volume.

Capillaries Smallest of the blood vessels, the site of exchange between the tissues and the blood.

Capillary Bed Network of capillaries served by one arteriole.

Capillary Exchange Exchange of oxygen and carbon dioxide in tissue capillaries. Oxygen diffuses from red blood cells to tissue cells; carbon dioxide diffuses in the opposite direction from tissue cells to red blood cells.

Cardiac Muscle Type of muscle tissue found in the heart.

Cardiac Output Volume of blood ejected by each ventricle in one minute. Computed by multiplying the heart rate by the stroke volume.

Cardiovascular System *See* **Circulatory System.**

Chemoreceptiors Special cells that detect chemicals.

Circulatory System Consists of the heart, blood, and blood vessels. Delivers nutrients and oxygen to the tissues.

Glossary

Clotting Factors Enzymes that trigger the blood-clotting cascade.

Coagulation The blood-clotting process.

Congestive Heart Failure Failure of the heart to pump blood effectively, causing blood to accumulate in the lungs.

Cooperative Binding The principle that the binding of one substrate molecule increases the ability to bind more substrate molecules.

Coronary Arteries The arteries that provide oxygen and nutrients to the heart muscle.

Deoxyhemoglobin Hemoglobin that has no oxygen bound to it.

Desmosomes Adhesion proteins that tightly bind cardiac muscle fibers together.

Diastole Relaxation of the heart between its contractions; opposite of systole.

Diffusion Random movement of molecules from a region of high concentration to one of low concentration.

Electrocardiogram (ECG or **EKG)** Graphic record of heart's action potentials.

Eosinophils A type of granulocyte (white blood cell) that fights parasitic infections.

Erythrocytes *See* **Red Blood Cells.**

Erythropoietin Hormone produced in the kidneys that stimulates the production of red blood cells.

Fibrin Protein strands that stabilize a blood clot.

Filtration Passage of water and solutes through a membrane from hydrostatic pressure.

Gap Junctions Openings that link the cytoplasm of one cell with that of another, found in cardiac muscle cells.

Globin Globular protein component of hemoglobin and other molecules.

Globulins A class of blood plasma proteins; includes antibodies.

Heart Attack Condition that occurs when the blood supply to part of the heart muscle (the myocardium) is reduced or stopped due to blockage of one or more of the coronary arteries. Also known as a myocardial infarction.

Heart Rate Initiated in the sinoatrial (SA) node of the heart, the rate at which the heart contracts and relaxes.

Hematocrit Percent volume of red blood cells in blood.

Hematopoiesis Production of the formed elements of the blood.

Hematopoietic Stem Cells Immature cells found in the bone marrow that give rise to white and red blood cells and platelets.

Heme Nonprotein, iron-containing component of hemoglobin.

Hemoglobin Respiratory pigment that binds oxygen, found in red blood cells.

Hemophilia Class of hereditary blood-clotting disorders.

Hemorrhage Bleeding.

Hypergravity Gravity greater than that on Earth.

Inferior Vena Cava The major vein returning blood from the lower body regions to the heart.

Intercalated Discs Tight connections between cardiac muscle fibers.

Kwashiorkor Protein-deficiency disease characterized by swelling of the abdomen.

Leukocytes *See* **White Blood Cells.**

Lymphocytes Type of leukocyte, or white blood cell, involved in immune function.

Megakaryocytes Precursor cells that give rise to platelets.

Microgravity Near-zero gravity or weightlessness; gravity that is much lower than Earth's gravity.

Monocytes White blood cells that develop into macrophages, phago-cytosing infectious agents.

Myocardial Infarction Medical term for heart attack.

Neutrophils An abundant type of granulocyte (white blood cell) that fights infection.

Orthostatic Intolerance A condition in which dizziness is experienced upon standing up, typically due to low blood pressure.

P Wave A deflection wave of an ECG; represents the depolarization of the atria.

Glossary

Pacemaker Cells Cells of the SA node that are autorhythmic.

Plaque Patch-like deposit of cholesterol that forms on the walls of blood vessels.

Plasma The liquid, noncellular portion of the blood.

Platelets Cell fragments found in the blood involved in the clotting process.

Polymorphonuclear granulocytes A class of white blood cells that reveal a multilobed nucleus when stained. Includes the eosinophils, the basophils, and the neutrophils.

Precapillary Sphincters Muscular openings to capillary beds.

Prothrombin Inactive form of the blood enzyme thrombin.

Pulmonary Circuit The portion of the circulatory system that supplies blood to the lungs.

Pulmonary Semilunar Valve Heart valve that separates the right ventricle from the pulmonary trunk, or aorta.

Purkinje Fibers Branching cardiac muscle that originates from the atrioventricular bundle in the atrioventricular (AV) node, extending out to the papillary muscles and lateral walls of the ventricles.

QRS Complex Represents depolarization of the ventricles on an ECG.

Reabsorption Process of absorbing fluid again.

Red Blood Cells The cells of the blood that contain the respiratory pigment hemoglobin and deliver oxygen to the body tissues. Also known as erythrocytes.

Resistance Vessels Blood vessels that affect blood pressure by increasing or decreasing their diameters.

Respiratory Pump Contractions of the diaphragm through normal respiration that increase the pressure gradient between peripheral veins and vena cavae, thereby promoting the return of venous blood to the heart.

Saturation Curve The graphic representation of the relationship between the oxygen concentration of the environment and the degree of saturation of a molecule like hemoglobin with oxygen.

Serum Blood plasma without its clotting proteins.

Sinoatrial Node Also known as the SA node, the region within the right atrium of the heart that generates the heart rhythm.

Skeletal Muscle Pump "Booster" pump for the heart, promoting venous blood return to the heart through contractions of skeletal muscles.

Stroke Volume Volume of blood pumped out of the ventricles by each heartbeat.

Superior Vena Cava The major vein returning blood from the upper body regions to the heart.

Systemic Circuit The portion of the circulatory system that supplies the systemic tissues (all tissues except the lungs).

Systole Contraction of the heart muscle.

T Wave A deflection wave of an ECG. Represents repolarization (relaxation) of the ventricles.

Tachycardia Abnormally rapid heart rate.

Thrombin Blood enzyme that triggers fibrin formation during the blood-clotting process.

Tricuspid Valve Alternative name for the right atrioventricular valve.

Universal Donor Blood Type Blood that is O negative—that is, blood containing neither A nor B antigens, which can be donated to individuals of any blood type.

Universal Recipient Blood Type Blood that is AB positive—that is, blood containing both A and B antigens on the surface of its red blood cells. AB positive blood can receive transfusions from any other blood type.

Vasoconstrict Decrease the diameter of a blood vessel.

Vasodilate Increase the diameter of a blood vessel.

Vasomotion Pulsatile blood flow observed within capillary beds.

Venous Return Movement of blood back to the heart.

Ventricles Chambers of the heart that pump blood into circulation.

Venules Small veins that collect blood leaving the capillaries.

White Blood Cells The cells of the blood that fight infection and disease, also known as leukocytes.

Bibliography and Further Reading

Behar, M. "Defying gravity." *Scientific American.* (March 2002). Available at *http://www.sciam.com/print.*

David, L. "Artificial gravity and space travel." *Bioscience.* 42 (1992).

"Emergency rooms to experiment with artificial blood." *CNN Interactive.* (February 17, 1997). Available at *http://www.cnn.com/HEALTH/9702/17/nfm/ artificial.blood.*

Ferber, D. "Out of this world physiology." *The Scientist.* (December 6, 2001). Available at *http://www.bio-medcentral.com/news/20011206/03.*

Grigor'ev, A.I., and B.M. Federov. "Current problems of Space Medicine and Physiology." *Human Physiology.* 24 (1998): 724–27.

Lewis, R. *Human Genetics: Concepts and Applications*, 3rd ed. New York: WCB McGraw-Hill, 1999.

Martini, F.H. *Fundamentals of Anatomy and Physiology*, 4th ed. Upper Saddle River, N.J.: Prentice Hall, 1998.

"New recommendations for blood pressure." National Heart, Lung, and Blood Institute report. 2003.

"NHLBI Issues New High Blood Pressure Clinical Practice Guidelines." *NIH News.* May 14, 2003. Available at *http://www.nhlbi.nih.gov/new/press/nhlbi-06.htm.*

Saladin, K. *Anatomy and Physiology: The Unity of Form and Function*, 1st ed. New York: WCB McGraw-Hill, 1998.

Shier, D., J. Butler, and R. Lewis. *Hole's Human Anatomy and Physiology*, 8th ed. New York: WCB McGraw-Hill Publishers, 1999.

Vander, A., J. Sherman, and D. Luciano. *Human Physiology: The Mechanism of Body Function*, 8th ed. New York: McGraw-Hill Publishers, 2001.

American Heart Association, Information about
  Atherosclerosis and Heart Attack
  www.americanheart.org

American Red Cross
  www.redcross.org

Ames Center for Gravitational Biology, NASA
  http://lifesci.arc.nasa.gov

National Heart, Lung, And Blood Institute
  www.nhlbi.nih.gov

National Women's Health Information Center
  www.4women.gov

Vanderbilt Center for Space Physiology and Medicine
  www.mc.vanderbilt.edu/gcrc/space/

Conversion Chart

Unit (metric)		Metric to English		English to Metric	
LENGTH					
Kilometer	km	1 km	0.62 mile (mi)	1 mile (mi)	1.609 km
Meter	m	1 m	3.28 feet (ft)	1 foot (ft)	0.305 m
Centimeter	cm	1 cm	0.394 inches (in)	1 inch (in)	2.54 cm
Millimeter	mm	1 mm	0.039 inches (in)	1 inch (in)	25.4 mm
Micrometer	μm				
WEIGHT (MASS)					
Kilogram	kg	1 kg	2.2 pounds (lbs)	1 pound (lbs)	0.454 kg
Gram	g	1 g	0.035 ounces (oz)	1 ounce (oz)	28.35 g
Milligram	mg				
Microgram	μg				
VOLUME					
Liter	L	1 L	1.06 quarts	1 gallon (gal)	3.785 L
				1 quart (qt)	0.94 L
				1 pint (pt)	0.47 L
Milliliter	mL or cc	1 mL	0.034 fluid ounce (fl oz)	1 fluid ounce (fl oz)	29.57 mL
Microliter	μL				
TEMPERATURE					
$°C = 5/9 \ (°F - 32)$		$°F = 9/5 \ (°C + 32)$			

Index

Index

page:

11: Lambda Science Artwork
18: Lambda Science Artwork
24: Lambda Science Artwork
26: Lambda Science Artwork
27: Lambda Science Artwork
29: Lambda Science Artwork
31: Lambda Science Artwork
37: Lambda Science Artwork
39: Lambda Science Artwork
42: © Dr. Stanley Flegler/Visuals Unlimited
44: Lambda Science Artwork
47: Lambda Science Artwork

51: Lambda Science Artwork
52: Lambda Science Artwork
53: Lambda Science Artwork
55: © Dr. Fred Hossler/Visuals Unlimited
55: Lambda Science Artwork
61: Lambda Science Artwork
63: Lambda Science Artwork
64: Lambda Science Artwork
66: Lambda Science Artwork
70: Lambda Science Artwork
81: Lambda Science Artwork
85: Lambda Science Artwork

About the Author

Dr. Susan Whittemore is a Professor of Biology at Keene State College in Keene, NH. She received a Master's degree from Utah State University and her Ph.D. in Physiology from Dartmouth Medical School in 1991. She also completed a postdoctoral program in molecular endocrinology at Dartmouth before arriving at Keene State in 1993. Dr. Whittemore teaches a wide range of biology courses for nonmajors, including Genetics and Society, Forensic Science, Women and Science, Human Biology, and Human Anatomy and Physiology. In addition, she teaches an introductory Biology course, Research Rotations, Physiology of Plants and Animals, Comparative Animal Physiology, and Ecophysiology. She was a recent recipient of an NSF grant that provided instrumentation for her work in molecular physiology. She was a contributing author to Scott Freeman's *Biological Sciences* (2002), an introductory biology text published by Prentice Hall.